TO

....

FROM

....

DATE

....

to the girl

LOOKING
FOR

more

90 DEVOTIONS TO HELP YOU **DITCH THE LIES,**
LOVE YOURSELF, AND **LIVE BIG FOR GOD**

GRACE VALENTINE

An Imprint of Thomas Nelson

To all the teachers and educators from kindergarten to college who made me the woman I am today. Thank you for being patient with me, educating me, seeing me, and helping me to always remember I can do anything in this world. It's because of teachers like you that young women can realize they are meant for more.

Ms. Freemen, Ms. Hebert, Ms. Gieg, Ms. Fisher, Ms. Peterson, Ms. Oynes, Ms. Benton, Ms. Amato, Ms. Wolf, Ms. Posey, Ms. Dendinger, Ms. Vicknair, Ms. Jordan/Tully, Ms. Rhodus, Ms. Este, Ms. Jarrell, Ms. Messenger, Mr. Delouche, Ms. Parker, Ms. Easterling, Ms. Carly, Ms. Hulon, Coach Hunt, Ms. Priebe, Ms. Hebert, Ms. Sisney, Ms. Matherne, Ms. Driscoll, Mr. Vitrano, Ms. Stacy, Prof. Tankersley, Prof. Perry, Dr. Mia-Moody Ramirez, and of course Dr. Burleson.

I am forever thankful for you all.

CONTENTS

PRAISE FOR *TO THE GIRL LOOKING FOR MORE*

"*To the Girl Looking for More* is truly a survival guide for every young woman. It uses both Scripture and Grace's relatable stories to remind all women of their worth, value, and purpose."

MADISON PREWETT TROUTT, AUTHOR OF *MADE FOR THIS MOMENT*

"Through humor and scripture, Grace Valentine delivers a devotional that will surely bless so many. She has a way of making young women feel seen, while also pointing them to Christ. Girls will relate to Grace in this devotional and leave compelled to live big for God."

ELISABETH HASSELBECK, *NEW YORK TIMES* BESTSELLING AUTHOR, EMMY AWARD-WINNING TALK SHOW HOST, MOM

"Grace Valentine is an incredibly gifted speaker and writer! Grace never fails to help out your everyday girl. This book will be sure to do the same. If you are looking for more out of your life and your walk with God, this is the book for you!"

JEANINE AMAPOLA, AUTHOR AND PODCAST HOST OF *HAPPY AND HEALTHY*

"*To the Girl Looking for More* is an honest, heartfelt, and relatable devotional that feels like a warm hug from a friend right when you need one. It is filled with empowering stories that will bring healing to hurting hearts and God's beautiful grace into your life!"

MEREDITH FOSTER, YOUTUBER AND DIGITAL CREATOR, @MEREDITHFOSTER

"This devotional is the empowering best friend that every girl needs, and it will leave you with a full heart that is ready to live for God. Grace and this book are a true blessing!"

CAMBREE, HIGH SCHOOL STUDENT

"Grace Valentine is the big sister this next generation needs. She's relatable, fun, and intuitive, speaking to the secret struggles of teenage girls through real-life stories and Scripture. I love Grace's heart, and this devotional is her best work yet. I can't wait to recommend it and buy copies for my daughters!"

KARI KAMPAKIS, BESTSELLING AUTHOR OF *LOVE HER WELL* AND HOST OF THE *GIRL MOM* PODCAST

"Grace's work always makes me feel like I'm getting a hug from an older sister. Grace's writing is real. Her work is vulnerable and genuine, and I can't help but picture myself in her stories. She doesn't try to act like she has everything together, and it's refreshing to read an author's work and not feel bad about myself. Thank you, Grace, for making all of us feel seen."

KEMBREE, HIGH SCHOOL STUDENT

"In some way, us girls are *all* wanting more. And who better to share their heart on this topic than Grace Valentine—a girl who has *found* more. Grace Valentine is filled with love for God, His girls, and His grace as we each run the unique race set before us. Her stories say honestly, "I've been there, sis, and I see you." Grace is the big sister I've always wanted. Open these pages, and you'll find a friend you didn't know you needed."

GEORGIA BROWN, AUTHOR AND SINGER-
SONGWRITER, @IAMGEORGIABROWN

"This book will be one I continue to purchase for the females in my life! These pages contain encouragement and truth for everyone as the Lord uses Grace's words to speak to every reader."

MADISON WEEKS, CREATOR OF ME TOO, SISTER, @METOOSISTER

"Grace is someone who always makes you feel at home—and this devotional does exactly that. It has it all: real stories, genuine advice, Scripture, and prayer. This book is a breath of fresh air and something I will recommend to anyone looking to dive deeper into their faith, while learning to rejoice in our imperfections."

SYDNEY STONE, AUBURN UNIVERSITY STUDENT

"Grace Valentine makes me feel accepted, understood, and valued for who I am in every phase and season of my life. And this devotional is her best work. God's light shines so brightly through her passionate words and vivid storytelling, and He is using her to guide girls and women toward Him."

ANNA BRADLEY BLACK, MISSISSIPPI STATE UNIVERSITY STUDENT

"Grace is refreshingly relatable. She's the big sister and mentor I wish I had growing up and helps you see that through trial or triumph, everything points to Jesus. The gentle reminders to pursue holiness give you the confidence and motivation to live for Christ."

NICOLE RENARD, TIKTOK CREATOR, MISS WASHINGTON 2017, @NICOLE_THENOMAD

"What I love about Grace is her relatability, humor, and ability to feel what her readers are feeling. Whether she's talking about the struggles of college or getting real about being a Christian in a world that isn't following Jesus, her words are refreshing and healing for the soul. If you are a young woman trying to follow God and you truly want MORE for your life, this book is for you."

ASHLEY HETHERINGTON, AUTHOR, FOUNDER OF @THEHONEYSCOOP

"Grace Valentine has written not only the book I needed as a young woman, but one that I'll be recommending to everyone I know. A combination of best friend, big sister, and wise teacher, Grace's heart pours out in this must-have book that covers it all."

"*To the Girl Looking for More* is a beautiful collection of mini books that any female can relate to. Grace is so real and reminds us that we have only one purpose: Jesus."

"Grace's devotional touches on topics that young ladies struggle with on a daily basis. As a mom of a high school senior, it is important to me to have a place for my daughter to turn that will lead her in truth and biblical guidance to help her overcome her tough days. Thank you, Grace, for being real for our daughters."

"Grace Valentine's words are a difference maker. She speaks to young women right where they're living, and she talks about the things that matter most to them without a hint of legalism or judgment. I've lost count of how many times I've heard young women mention that Grace feels like a trusted friend to them, and my response is always the same: *that's because she is.* *To the Girl Looking for More* is a devotional book that is life-giving, encouraging, understanding, practical, and most importantly, overflowing with hope. It's a safe place for girls to examine and process the deepest questions and concerns of their hearts, and it will be an invaluable companion in the lives of so many. Well done, Grace. Your writing is a gift to women of all ages! (Also, I am super proud of you. And I am proud of myself for not using the word "grace" as a pun in this review.)"

"As a 20-year-old girl who still has no clue what she wants to do with her life, I do know one thing after reading *To the Girl Looking for More*: my heart is on fire for Jesus! Grace is an author who not only recognizes the magical and sparkly moments of life but also the real and raw ones. There is a truthful and faithful heart behind each of these pages."

Hello, friend!

I can't help but wonder where you are today as you start this devotional. Are you in your bedroom with the bright teal paint you picked when you were ten, or are you in a messy dorm room? Are you in a city with food trucks and skyscrapers, in the suburbs where there's one mediocre Mexican restaurant, or out in the country? Is it chilly, or are you down south, like where I grew up?

But what I really want to know is where you are mentally. Have your classes this year made you feel worthless, or has a boy just broken your heart? Are you lonely during lunch? Is the party scene making you feel worse? Are you stressed about the future or living for others' approval?

Sit with me, little sister, and let's chat. We'll put on some old Taylor Swift songs, pile the pillows on your bed, and talk about all of it. We'll talk about your stress, anxious thoughts, rejection, shame, and hurt. We'll talk about the friend who left you and the pressure to pick a major or career.

Then let me tell you one important truth: YOU ARE MEANT FOR MORE. The world tells girls to *be more*: be more beautiful, be more Christian, be more like her, be busier . . . And we try *so hard*.

God gave you that desire for more, but He wants you to experience true satisfaction in your hollow, weary heart. He wants you to have more love in your relationships, more peace, more purpose, more contentment, more self-love, more joy, and, most of all, more of Him.

I used to be like you, looking for fullness as life kept leaving me empty. I've been the girl who got bullied, the girl rejected from the job, the girl whose friends created a group text without her, the girl who drank too much, the girl who went too far with a guy, the girl who felt pressure to prove herself.

But that's not me anymore. I finally realized that I have a Savior who sees me, with all my baggage and blemishes, and says that my life is meant for more than beauty, romance, achievement, or popularity. If you're looking for an author who has it all together, this book isn't for you. I've learned lessons the hard way, kissed frogs, felt the weight of body image, and struggled with mental health. But if you're looking for an author who is honest, maybe this book will help you stop looking for, and start finding, MORE.

I can share what I've learned and show you that God is real and that He cares for you. I hope that, with me by your side, you can grow closer to our great God and find your more. But remember that you can't do this on your own. Some problems are especially hard, or even dangerous, and I want to encourage you to seek help. Find someone a couple steps ahead of you that you trust, talk to a counselor, or reach out to a local church. There are people ready to help you. God doesn't want you to go through your hard alone. Be bold and ask for help.

So wherever you are right now, do yourself a favor. Take the pressure off. This world is demanding more from you, but it can't provide the purpose and answers you're seeking. There is a Savior right beside you, and He's ready to show you what He meant this life to be. As you spend time in this devotional, I hope you'll meet your Savior. He is the more you've been looking for.

xoxo, grace valentine

GOD
CELEBRATES
HEARTS THAT

seek Him.

More

PURPOSE

TO THE GIRL SEEKING PURPOSE

"Martha, Martha," the Lord answered, "you are worried
and upset about many things, but few things are
needed—or indeed only one. Mary has chosen what
is better, and it will not be taken away from her."

—LUKE 10:41–42

I used to have an addiction to saying yes. *Yes* was my most used word. If someone asked me to lead a club, work their shift, help them study, go to a party, join the team . . . I would say yes. I thought that to find more purpose I had to say yes more. But I only became more busy.

I get that you do this too. You say yes more than you should, and you live busy more than you live purposefully. However, Jesus never asked you to be busy.

There's a Bible passage I love from the story of Mary and Martha, sisters who hosted Jesus in their home. They each handled His visit differently. Martha cleaned the house and cooked a meal. Mary sat at Jesus' feet and listened to Him. Martha got mad that her sister wasn't helping with the work. But Jesus told Martha, "You are worried and upset about many things, but few things are needed—or indeed only one." Martha was being productive, but she was missing out on her purpose. What Martha was doing was helpful—but it wasn't holy.

Don't let your plans distract you from your purpose. There's nothing wrong with having plans. But are you pursuing plans, or are you pursuing purpose? I often get distracted from God's will when I focus on my will. My will is to be busy, have plans, be productive, and achieve success. But God's will is for me to pursue my relationship with Him.

You have only one purpose, and it is Jesus: To love Jesus. To be with Jesus. To show others Jesus.

So, today I say to my busy, overwhelmed, tired friend: drop your to-do list. Drop your plans if they are getting in the way of time with Jesus. Jesus doesn't want your schedule, your GPA, your popularity, your hustle, or your good deeds. Jesus wants *you*. Make time for Jesus. Be with Jesus. Call out to Him, then give Him your silence so He has a chance to speak.

How are you supposed to figure out your purpose if you aren't doing life with the One who created you? How are you supposed to change the world if you're not first sitting at the feet of the One who saved the world? You can work as hard as you want, but if you aren't sitting at His feet, you're missing out on true purpose.

Dear God, You never called me to say yes to everyone. You called me to know You and sit at Your feet. Help me be more aware of Your presence than I am of my to-do list. Amen.

TO THE GIRL WANTING TO DO BIG THINGS

"Come," he said.
Then Peter got down out of the boat, walked
on the water and came toward Jesus. But when
he saw the wind, he was afraid and, beginning
to sink, cried out, "Lord, save me!"

—MATTHEW 14:29–30

Like most students home from college, I spent Christmas break my freshman year napping, avoiding my middle school bullies, and stressing about the future. I wanted to find purpose. But I kept getting distracted by what "made sense," what wasn't "too crazy," and fear of failure.

While I was home, I met up with an old mentor named Ms. Stacy. "I really want to write books," I told her. "But I know that sounds crazy."

She looked at me and said, "I see it." Ms. Stacy saw more than the girl sitting on her couch. She saw my potential, and she believed in me.

Your own dream may seem crazy, but the Lord says to you, "I see it. I see your potential. Be bold, and take a step toward Me."

You can do big things if you look at your big God. Trust that the calling God has placed on your heart is there for a reason. It's not for money, success, fame, or proud parents. God gave you this passion so you can glorify Him and step toward His purpose for you.

Like me, you probably have fears about failing. I can't promise your dream will happen the way you want. God might have something different for you. HE DOESN'T PROMISE SUCCESS; HE PROMISES HIS PRESENCE.

Peter was a dreamer too. He was a disciple, someone who followed Jesus around when He was on earth. During a storm one night, Jesus' disciples were in a boat. They had left Jesus on shore, but suddenly they saw Him walking on the water. All the other disciples were scared. But Peter did something crazy.

Peter got out of the boat and walked on the water toward Jesus. Was leaving the boat smart? No—there was a freaking storm going on! But Peter chose closeness to Jesus over comfort in the boat. He stepped out and did the unthinkable!

However, when he looked at the wind, he sank. When you look at what makes sense, others' expectations, or your fear, you'll sink. Instead, look forward to your big God. I know you dream of doing big things. You want a walk-on-water life. You want to do the unthinkable. That's great. Chase crazy and leave the boat. Step toward Jesus.

Dear God, help me look past the distractions and look at You. Remind me of Your power on the days I doubt myself and my dreams feel crazy. Remind me that my steps are not for results but to get closer to You. Change my heart so I don't crave success but instead crave to bring You glory. I want to step toward You. Amen.

TO THE GIRL FEELING DISAPPOINTED

"For I know the plans I have for you," declares
the LORD, "plans to prosper you and not to harm
you, plans to give you hope and a future."
—JEREMIAH 29:11

When I was in eighth grade, I was good at math. So I placed in an advanced math class, and throughout high school my mom insisted I take all the hard math classes. But as the math got harder, everyone seemed to get smarter except me. My senior year, I took business calculus. I tried so hard and even met with my teacher individually, but I still struggled. I remember staying up until 3 a.m. one night trying to learn the patterns and methods for a big test. The next day, I left the test actually feeling good about it. But then my grade came in. I got a 37.

Disappointment happens to everyone. Your disappointment might come from a text with no reply, a friend who betrays you, a breakup, or a divorce. And if you're like me, it will leave you with puffy eyes and ruined mascara—in the middle of math class. And then you'll be disappointed in yourself for not keeping it together.

But when you're disappointed that life isn't going the way you want, remember: YOU AREN'T THE AUTHOR OF YOUR STORY. You may have wanted a comma where God placed a period. You may have wanted a chapter to close, but God kept writing it. Your disappointment may make you cry, but never allow it to stop you from believing that the Lord has a plan for you.

God is writing a better story than you could ever fathom. It isn't better because you'll get the cool guy and go to the nice formal. It isn't better because you'll get the clout and viral moment. It's better because you'll get His presence. His plan isn't always your plan—it's better. Knowing who Jesus is and letting Him direct your steps helps you see the tears for what they are: a passing bump in the road that will point you in the right direction. Because when you know that your God is a good Author, you can trust that the disappointment in your current chapter is leading to where you're supposed to be.

Four years after I cried about my 37, I saw my senior math teacher again. She was kind and told me, "There was a good plan for you—it just didn't involve math." She was so right.

Your tears today are simply a trial leading you to your blessings. Trust this. His plans are giving you a hope and a future. My future didn't involve math. I passed business calculus with a C. That was my worst grade that year, but I passed. I never had to take another math class, and God led me to a major that required more writing than calculus. God knew what He was doing.

Dear God, I feel disappointed. Help me trust in Your plan. Thank You for being the Author of my story. I am hurt, but I am also loved by You. Amen.

TO THE GIRL WHO HAS
BEEN THROWN OUT

"My God sent his angel, and he shut the mouths of the lions.
They have not hurt me, because I was found innocent in his
sight. Nor have I ever done any wrong before you, Your Majesty."

—DANIEL 6:22

There's this old Katy Perry song called "Firework." In one of the lines, she asks if you've ever felt like a plastic bag floating on the breeze, wishing for a new start. I remember listening to this song nonstop on YouTube when I was in high school. And I've thought about this lyric even recently. As cheesy as it is, I relate to it.

I have felt thrown out by guys who ghosted me, girls who used me to get to my friends and then left me out, a job that overworked me only to furlough me, friends' moms who drove me home from church and then gossiped about me like I was a reality-show star, and friends who abandoned me. There have even been times when I felt like God was avoiding me. The truth is, others may use you and then reject you, but God is always there, making a way. He will help you start again. And when you feel like a plastic bag, used once and then thrown out, remind yourself that God is protecting you. When you find Him in the pain, you'll find purpose. He will remind you that you were never a piece of trash. You are His child.

In the Bible, we learn about Daniel, who was an adviser to an important king. But because Daniel prayed to God, the king threw him in the lions' den. However, when Daniel was in the den, God shut the lions' mouths and didn't let them hurt Daniel. He survived and proclaimed that God had protected him. Then the whole area came to know of God.

You may feel like you've been thrown in the lions' den, but have no fear. Your God is protecting you, and your God will meet you where you are. Your struggle is real, but you can use it to help others know who He is. Your response to your struggle can point to Christ's miracles. It is so easy to feel thrown out, but sometimes you're really being thrown into a miracle.

Dear Father, thank You for having the power to save me from whatever trouble I'm thrown into. When I feel pushed aside or I'm struggling, help me see that You are making miracles in the crazy. Help me be bold for You even when I feel pushed aside. Amen.

TO THE GIRL FEELING STUCK

So then, let us rid ourselves of everything that gets in
the way, and of the sin which holds on to us so tightly,
and let us run with determination the race that lies
before us. Let us keep our eyes fixed on Jesus, on
whom our faith depends from beginning to end.

—HEBREWS 12:1–2 GNT

There's a story I don't want any boy to know about me. So in typical Grace Valentine fashion, I'll share it here and trust that you won't tell any eligible bachelors.

I went to pick up a friend from the Orlando airport. This is a big airport, and the line to reach the arrivals is always long. In the pickup lanes, there's a whistle lady. She works for the airport, and her whistle reminds people to keep moving and not leave their cars unattended.

I was early, but I was managing to avoid the whistle lady. Then it happened: I had a sensation of urgency in my tummy, and I knew I needed to poop. But I was stuck in my car. I tried to hold it in. I really did.

So yes, I pooped my pants. It was as gross as you can imagine. And there is nothing more humbling than pooping your pants.

Anyway, I say this to tell you: sometimes you feel stuck. You feel like you can't escape the hurt or the boredom. You wonder if you'll ever get where you want to be. Sometimes you feel like you're in the worst place at the worst time.

But guess what? You aren't stuck. YOU ARE FREE TO WALK BOLDLY INTO THE FUTURE GOD HAS FOR YOU. No one is forcing you to stay in a bad situation. Even if there is a whistle lady in your life—someone who will call you out or embarrass you—she can't make you stay. And any discomfort she can cause is nothing compared to staying where you aren't meant to be. I felt forced to stay in the car, but I could have pulled over and run inside. You don't need to wait on anyone to turn your life around.

And know this: God is never going to trap you. He's not blocking you in. In this season you may feel like it is impossible to find friendships, acceptance, or purpose. But you aren't truly stuck. You don't have to stay in a hurtful friendship—you can walk away. You don't have to stay in the party scene—you can choose obedience and peace.

God gave you free will so you can choose to follow Him. You can choose boldness over fear. Don't be stuck, be bold. Get rid of the fear and anything that hinders you from running boldly.

Dear God, no matter what I feel stuck in, I pray that I will be bold. Give me the courage to not be afraid. Give me the courage to walk away from anything that is not from You. Amen.

TO THE GIRL FEELING SHAME

And Peter remembered the word of the Lord, how He
had told him, "Before a rooster crows today, you will deny
Me three times." And he went out and wept bitterly.

—LUKE 22:61–62 NASB

When I was seventeen years old, a cute boy liked me—*me!* For a girl who was so insecure, this felt too good to be true. We started dating, and I did whatever made him happy. One night I crossed physical boundaries, even though I knew what I did was too far. I'll never forget the shame and regret I felt afterward.

I felt dirty. I felt unworthy. I felt stuck.

Is that you? Maybe you feel shame that you cheated on that test, or you regret the way you talked about a friend. Maybe you feel unworthy because of what you searched for on the internet. Yes, you sinned. But your God created grace. He gave you a Savior who not only forgives you but also wants more for you. He wants you to walk in purpose, not to be stuck in shame.

When we mess up, we need to be like Peter. Peter was best friends with Jesus, but he denied knowing Christ three times when Jesus was arrested.

Jesus had predicted this, down to the crowing rooster, but Peter had promised that he would *never*. After Peter betrayed Jesus, he wept.

But what made Peter cry wasn't shame; it was conviction. Shame makes you hide from God. But Peter *ran* to look for Jesus when he heard about the empty tomb (Luke 24:12). Peter wasn't stuck in shame. He was ready to move forward in forgiveness and purpose.

Sin *should* make us uncomfortable. You don't feel right after you mess up because you are not walking in God's best. When you walk in obedience, you may miss out on the hot gossip or the easy A. You may not have popular friends or get the guy. But you will have something better: purpose.

See, shame says that you're too dirty for Christ. Conviction says you can do better for Christ. What did Peter do next? After Jesus rose from the dead, Peter worked each day to share the good news of salvation. Conviction helped Peter walk in obedience and do great things.

Let go of shame and embrace conviction. Then accept Jesus' grace, turn away from sin, and tell others what God has done in you. When you walk in purpose despite your messy past, God will use your past as a tool to glorify Him. Your mistakes become your testimony.

Dear God, I want to be like Peter. Give me the boldness to leave shame behind and walk forward from conviction. My sin is messy, but I will not believe the lie that I am too dirty to serve You. I believe Your grace can change me and use me. I know I will mess up again, but help me to walk in conviction, turn away from shame, and find purpose with You. Amen.

TO THE GIRL READY TO MAKE A DIFFERENCE

"For if you remain silent at this time, relief and deliverance
for the Jews will arise from another place, but you and your
father's family will perish. And who knows but that you have
come to your royal position for such a time as this?"

—ESTHER 4:14

When I was twenty-five, I got a message from someone I met when I was sixteen. We had gone to the same youth-group retreat, and he was thanking me for sticking up for him. At the retreat some boys were calling him names, and I cut in and told the boys to stop. Then we hung out for the rest of the weekend, even though he was younger than me. I only vaguely remember this happening! But he remembered my words and invite a decade later.

And the truth is that I remember when my eighth-grade classmate stuck up for me when some boys were calling me names. Years later, I'm a bridesmaid in her wedding.

It's scary to speak up when you see something wrong. It's also scary to invite someone to church or talk to someone about Jesus. It's scary to be bold, but being bold is worth it. SPEAKING UP ISN'T EVEN ABOUT FINDING YOUR

VOICE, IT'S ABOUT FINDING YOUR LOVE. Love is an action. Loving well starts with boldness.

One of my favorite Bible stories is in the book of Esther. I could go on and on, but I'll summarize it real quick: A Jewish woman who was beautiful inside and out married a powerful king. Some annoying dude tried to kill all the Jewish people in the kingdom by tricking the king. Because of her position as queen, Esther had an opportunity to stand up for justice and save the Jews. She almost stayed quiet because she was terrified of speaking up to the king. She wasn't perfect, but she followed God's purpose for her and spoke up. And spoiler alert: God used her to save the people!

My favorite thing about this story is the quote from Esther's uncle in chapter 4. When he found out about the plan to kill the Jews, he begged Esther to go to the king. He told her that God put her in her position "for such a time as this." You, too, are placed in your small town, in your class, in your big apartment complex, in your family—for a reason. God placed you there for a purpose, and He is giving you opportunities to make a difference right where you are. Look around. What do you need to stand up for? Who can you love?

Dear God, use my position for Your purpose. Help me to be bold and speak up about my faith, to stand up for what is right, and to act out love. I believe Your Word that I am here "for such a time as this." Amen.

5 WAYS TO MAKE A DIFFERENCE

1. BE WHO YOU NEEDED WHEN YOU WERE YOUNGER. YOUR PAST TRIALS CAN BE SOMEONE ELSE'S SURVIVAL GUIDE.

2. SHOW EVERYONE WHO THEIR BIG GOD IS BY LIVING OUT OF KINDNESS AND LOVE, NOT SELFISHNESS.

3. WRITE A LETTER, TALK TO A STRANGER, CHECK ON A FRIEND. SMALL ACTS OF LOVE ARE POWERFUL.

4. USE WHAT GOD HAS GIVEN YOU TO LOVE OTHERS. YOU HAVE UNIQUE GIFTS AND PASSIONS THAT GOD CREATED FOR A REASON.

5. SEE OTHERS THE WAY JESUS SEES THEM.

WHO KNOWS BUT THAT YOU HAVE
COME TO YOUR ROYAL POSITION

FOR SUCH A TIME AS THIS?

—ESTHER 4:14

TO THE GIRL WANTING A MAIN-CHARACTER LIFE

Peter went with them, and when he arrived he was taken
upstairs to the room. All the widows stood around him,
crying and showing him the robes and other clothing
that [Tabitha] had made while she was still with them.

—ACTS 9:39

I used to think I was one talent scout away from being a movie star or that I was one royal grandma away from being a princess. Clearly, I watched too many Disney movies and shows.

When I got older, I did the same thing with the "cool girl" life. I just knew I could be popular. All I needed was the coolest TikTok recap, the hot boyfriend and trendy friends, and a color-coded life—from my Instagram feed to my room to my wardrobe. But that picture-perfect princess isn't me. The most exciting things about me are my most embarrassing moments. Also, I can't sing or dance.

I bet you have struggled with this "main character" desire too. But in this desire for magic and stardom, we forget our purpose.

There was a woman in the Bible named Tabitha. There's almost nothing written about her other than that she loved Jesus and made clothes for the poor. And that she died. Two people brought Peter to Tabitha's body, which had been laid out in a room. When Peter got there, people were around her crying. They showed Peter the clothes Tabitha had sewed for them. Then Peter prayed for her, and Tabitha got up. She had been dead, but she was alive because of Jesus' power through Peter.

When I think of this passage, I smile. There's not much info about Tabitha. We don't know if she could sing or if she killed it as a boss girl. We will never know if she was considered beautiful. We do know that she cared for the overlooked. When she died, those she served were around her wearing the love and kindness she gave them.

I get it. I do. You want to be all the things, and that's normal. I hope you kill it at school and work, run that 10k, and decorate your room all cute. But remember that the most meaningful thing you can do is love the overlooked. When you die, no one will care if your TikTok went viral or if you looked like a Zara model. People will remember how you made them feel.

So take a deep breath and remember that you aren't the main character. But your Savior is. Be content with the beauty that comes from playing a supporting role in His story of love instead of living to prove you're worth loving.

Dear God, help me be content to love instead of trying to prove that I'm worth loving. Shift my perspective so my goal is to support Your story by loving the overlooked instead of seeking attention. Help me love like Tabitha today and always. Amen.

9

TO THE GIRL WONDERING WHY SHE IS HERE

*For in him all things were created: things in heaven
and on earth, visible and invisible, whether thrones
or powers or rulers or authorities; all things have
been created through him and for him.*

—COLOSSIANS 1:16

During junior year of high school, I took a career test. I selected my skills, desires, and dreams in little matching questions. The end of the test revealed my perfect career . . . mail carrier. Honestly, I would love to deliver mail. However, I am the worst driver. Imagine how many curbs I would hit with that cute little car! I knew that was not what I was meant to be.

And anyway, mail carriers don't make much money, and I wanted to be rich. I thought that to have purpose I had to be well off. So when people asked me what I wanted to be when I grew up, I named careers I thought would make money. Deep down I knew I wasn't put on this earth just to buy nice things. But as a girl who needed a job at fifteen, I thought being rich was important.

The problem with that idea is I love to write. And writing about Jesus doesn't make the money I had in mind. As I am writing this book, I'm also juggling two other jobs so I can pay my bills. I'm not rich, but I'm thankful that I chose to follow my purpose.

WALKING IN PURPOSE ISN'T ALWAYS PRETTY. Sometimes it's choosing a lower-paying job. Sometimes it's being the only one not cheating on the homework. Sometimes purpose is walking away from a relationship that isn't honoring God, and sometimes it's being okay with not knowing where you'll be in five years.

Maybe you don't know what you want to be. Or maybe you do know, but school is kicking your butt and you wonder if you can make it. Maybe you've been cast aside, and you wonder why you're here at all. Your purpose may not seem pretty or clear, but if you are a daughter of God, it is good. When we walk with the Lord, we may not have money, popularity, a perfect five-year plan, or fame. But we will have lives that make a difference. Your purpose is about something bigger than a job, a flush bank account, or a following of admirers. You're here for something bigger and for Someone better. You were created to know God and to make Him known by loving well.

There's no test that can predict where you'll be in five years. Your life may be confusing now, but God has a purpose for you. Talk to Him and live alongside Him. You'll discover His purpose at the right time. You're here for a reason.

Dear God, I struggle to know why I am here. But I understand that purpose comes from knowing You and loving big. Let all my choices—my college major, my career, my relationships—be choices that honor You. Amen.

TO THE GIRL WONDERING IF
HER IMPACT MATTERS

You will eat the fruit of your labor; blessings
and prosperity will be yours.

—PSALM 128:2

When I was sixteen, I helped continue a tradition my brother and his friends started. They had been leading a morning prayer time before school at Café Du Monde, a classic New Orleans café that serves coffee and beignets (a New Orleans pastry). After they graduated, I became one of the group leaders.

It was a fun group! Each week we cleaned up before we left for school, and I slowly began a relationship with the staff. They knew that on Thursday mornings we would be there: a bunch of public-school kids who were stressed about tests and silly relationships but were still starting our day by praying and reading the Bible. When I graduated, the staff even got me a gift.

However, the generation after me stopped coming. I tried to get younger leaders to step up, but it didn't work out. I felt like I failed in making a lasting difference for the younger students.

Five years later, a friend from the group told me she had gone to Café Du Monde and one of the workers remembered her and asked about me. Shortly after, I felt God tell me to stop by one morning when I was home. At first that seemed silly. What were the odds that the worker would have a shift that day, let alone have time to talk to me? I couldn't even remember her name.

But I felt God push me to walk in. The sweet worker was there, and she instantly recognized me. She even gave me a free breakfast! Then she told me that after seeing us come in weekly to read the Bible, she began to read the Bible too. Crazy, right? I had thought that my efforts to lead the study didn't have an impact. I hadn't even thought about the lady behind the register whom I'd assumed was busy and not listening.

Our impact isn't just for the people we see. Your kindness and faith can leave imprints on the hearts of all those you encounter. You may never see the full impact of your actions. But when you live out little acts of love consistently, you make the world better. So don't worry if you don't get the results or affirmation you expected. Follow God's lead and expect that He is working.

Just like a gardener must work hard before a sprout grows, work done in Christ's name will blossom into fruit. But it may not be the result or the way you expect. Stop seeking results, and instead, seek opportunities to share Christ's love with anyone.

Dear God, I pray my life impacts people. Help me love big—not for results or affirmation, but for You. Help me be faithful in the little things, whether a club, sport, leadership position, job, or babysitting gig. Use my efforts to bear Your fruit. Amen.

TO THE GIRL WONDERING WHAT
GOD IS CALLING HER TO

Jesus said to her, "Mary."
She turned toward him and cried out in Aramaic,
"Rabboni!" (which means "Teacher").

—JOHN 20:16

Picking a college major was daunting for me. The summer before college, I researched a bunch of majors trying to figure out which one I should pick. I prayed for clarity, and guess what I got? Nothing. No magical voice, no random encounter with a professor who told me I would do great on a prelaw track, and no "clarity."

By the week before I left for college, I was so stressed. I wanted to recognize God's hand and blessing on my decisions, but I just didn't hear Him. I was confused! Wasn't my major a big decision?

The truth is that I was praying for answers but not praying to spend time with Jesus. I was treating Jesus like a guidance counselor, wanting Him to reveal a five-year plan for me that made sense. But I was forgetting that

He is my Savior who knows my name, my gifts, and my worries. He knew my restless heart.

Once I stopped seeking an answer that came how I wanted, I saw my Savior who knew me by name. There was no lightning strike, and I didn't get any chills, but I felt God show me that He knew me. He reminded me that I like to write, so I chose journalism as my major. I wasn't sure if it was the perfect fit then, but it turned out to be exactly where God wanted me.

In the Bible, Mary Magdalene was the first person to see Jesus after He rose from the grave. She had gone to Jesus' tomb and saw that it was empty. She thought that someone had moved His body, so she started crying. Then she encountered a man she thought was a gardener—until that "gardener" said her name: "Mary." She realized the man was Jesus and that He was alive!

Sometimes in moments of confusion, you don't need your Savior to outline a plan. You just need to hear Him say your name. When you understand that your Savior is paying attention to you, you will have peace. Whether this is choosing a club, a major, a college or trade school, or even how to handle a fight with a friend, you may not need "clarity," you may just need to hear your Savior who knows your name.

Dear Jesus, I'm so glad You know my name. When I'm wondering what You're calling me to, may I remember to first seek You. Help me trust You even when I'm making hard decisions. You are my Savior and are walking with me. Amen.

12

TO THE GIRL WHO DOESN'T KNOW WHAT SHE WANTS TO BE WHEN SHE GROWS UP

Each of you should use whatever gift you have received to serve others, as faithful stewards of God's grace in its various forms.

—1 PETER 4:10

When I was little, I wanted to be an ice cream truck driver when I grew up. I thought being a driver would allow me to go in the back of the truck and eat all the ice cream. Then when I was around twelve, a show came out called *Hannah Montana* about a girl who was a famous pop star. She wore sparkly outfits, sang upbeat songs, and had the most fun wig. So I wanted to be a pop star too . . . even though I can't sing. As I got older, I dreamed of having lots of money and being known, so I told people I wanted to be a lawyer or a doctor.

There's a lot of pressure to have a perfect answer when someone asks you what you want to be when you grow up. You want to prove yourself and pick a career that makes you sound smart, fun, or important. But here's the truth: life isn't about knowing what's next or finding a career that makes your name known. A life of purpose is about realizing you are already known by your Savior.

You don't need to know what's next when you walk with the God who created you with unique gifts. He will lead you to where you are meant to be. So take a deep breath next time someone asks what you want to do one day. Remind yourself, and maybe them, too, that it is okay to not know. Instead of chasing a five-year plan for getting your dream career, seek self-knowledge. Look at the things you enjoy doing. What activity or study makes you feel closer to God? What are you good at? God has given you gifts. Explore your strengths, expand on your talents, and pray that God will open doors to opportunities that suit you. Your purpose is about more than your occupation, but God can and will use your occupation as part of your purpose.

The other key to discovering your next is to focus on making your Savior known, not on building a reputation for yourself. Don't worry about what job will impress others or bring a big check. Find peace in the truth that your God knows your giftings—He chose them just for you! And He can use any of your gifts to lead you to a job that will fill your soul and make a holy impact.

Dear God, I don't know what occupation will fit me best, but I trust that You know me. Will You reveal giftings You have given me that could lead me to a career? Help me use my future occupation as a tool to spread Your name and not as a means to prove myself or make my name known. Amen.

TO THE GIRL DISCERNING
HER NEXT MOVE

"When the people willingly offer themselves—praise the LORD!"

—JUDGES 5:2

In high school, I stressed about which college to attend. What if I picked the wrong one? What if I didn't go to the one that was best for me? After college, I worried about where to move. What if I picked a city that was horrible and hot and I made no friends?

I was trying to discern the best move. I wanted to choose the right college, the right city, the right everything. Surely there was a specific answer to each of these questions!

I think a lot of us try to discern one "right" answer to our situations. But no place is definitely wrong. There probably also isn't a "right" roommate or a "right" club or even a "right" friend. You can live for God wherever you are and whoever you're with. God wants you to focus on Him and stop trying to choose what's "best" or "right." THERE ISN'T ONE RIGHT WAY TO LIVE, BUT THERE IS A HOLY WAY. When you look to God for guidance and wisdom, you will find a good path.

There's a woman in the Bible named Deborah. Deborah was a leader of Israel. She was also a prophet, which means she was a teacher and proclaimer of God's will. Many people came to Deborah for advice. At the time, Israel was at war, and God gave Deborah a message for the army's leader, Barak. God wanted Barak to lead an attack, and God promised victory. But Barak was hesitant. He told Deborah, "If you go with me, I will go" (Judges 4:8). God didn't tell Deborah to fight, but she decided to join Barak in following God's directions to go to battle. She knew the fight would glorify God, and she wanted to be a part of it.

So now there's you. You have choices to make, and it is easy to stress about choosing wrong. But if you follow God and willingly offer Him your present and future, your steps will bring you closer to Him. And that's always right. Drop the pressure that comes from trying to do things "right." Instead, join God where He is working and choose good.

Dear Jesus, thank You that I don't have to stress about knowing one right choice. Help me offer my present and future to You and make holy choices. Guide me and show me where I can join the good things You are doing. Amen.

7 REMINDERS FOR THE GIRL READY TO WALK IN PURPOSE

1. GOD'S PURPOSE FOR YOU IS GREATER THAN YOUR PLAN.

2. IF YOU WANT TO DO SOMETHING BIG, YOU HAVE TO LOOK AT YOUR BIG GOD.

3. IT'S BETTER TO DO HOLY THINGS THAN MAIN-CHARACTER THINGS.

4. YOU WILL EXPERIENCE GOD'S BEST ONLY WHEN YOU'RE FOLLOWING HIM.

5. STOP TRYING TO PROVE THAT YOU'RE WORTH LOVING, AND BE LOVING.

6. YOU DON'T HAVE TO KNOW WHERE YOU ARE GOING. JUST REMEMBER WHO YOU ARE FOLLOWING.

7. LIFE ISN'T ABOUT PROVING THAT YOU'RE RIGHT; IT'S ABOUT POINTING OTHERS TO THE TRUTH.

More
SELF-WORTH

14

TO THE GIRL READY TO
LOVE HERSELF

But the fruit of the Spirit is love, joy, peace, patience,
kindness, goodness, faithfulness, gentleness, self-
control; against such things there is no law.
—GALATIANS 5:22–23 ESV

One day in seventh grade, I woke up with half my face paralyzed. And it was picture day.

When I smiled, only the left side of my face turned up. The right side was frozen. When I tried to raise my eyebrows, only half my forehead wrinkled. The other brow just sat there. And when I blinked, only one eye closed. I had a condition called Bell's palsy.

My condition lasted for about two months. That's considered a mild case of Bell's palsy, but it felt like forever. Being in seventh grade was hard enough without half my face deciding to take half the semester off! I was embarrassed and felt ugly. But God was teaching me that there are more important things than a good photo.

This wasn't the only time I struggled to love myself. As I grew older, I didn't like my voice—it was high-pitched. I wasn't as smart as I wanted to be—math was hard. And anytime I looked in the mirror, I didn't like what I saw. I hated who I was, and I felt like I wasn't worthy.

One day I woke up and thought, *This sucks.* But I realized what sucked wasn't my frizzy hair or my acne. It sucked that I couldn't love myself. I was ready to love myself, but I didn't know how.

Do you struggle with self-love? Are you finally ready to love *you*, as you are right now? Here are three things you can love yourself for:

Your character. Remember, the most beautiful things you can wear are the fruits of the Spirit. Patience is prettier than your outfit, and gentleness is a rare gem. Your legacy is your love, not your looks. Speak kindness to others. Look for the good in others, and you'll see the good in yourself.

Your body's purpose. Don't think, *I need body positivity!* Life isn't about being positive. It's about being purposeful. Remember, you're not a product to be enjoyed, you're a child of God walking on mission. Use your arms to hug your friends. Allow your feet to take you to volunteer opportunities. Work out to stay healthy, not to punish yourself. Celebrate what God can do with your body.

Your workmanship. You are beautiful not because of what you look like but because of who created you. And this Artist created you in the image of Himself. Don't fix what He calls beautiful and has named as His.

Dear God, help me see myself the way You see me. Remind me that I don't need positivity, I need purpose. The most beautiful thing I can do is walk with You in my heart. Help me live out the beauty of my salvation each day. Amen.

15

TO THE GIRL TOLD SHE ISN'T PRETTY

Thus says the LORD: "Cursed is the man who trusts in man and makes flesh his strength, whose heart turns away from the LORD."

—JEREMIAH 17:5 ESV

I used to feel like the ugly duckling. In middle school, I wore glasses from the same store that sold mayonnaise. My hair was frizzy, and I didn't have the best style. Some boys made fun of me and told me straight up that I was ugly. They said I would never get a boyfriend and trash-talked my looks.

When I was older, I was dating a guy for the first time. He'd had a girl-friend before me, and someone posted on social media that his ex-girlfriend was way prettier than me. Seeing the mean comment about my looks made me want to throw up. I lay awake that night watching the ceiling fan spin through my tears.

I used to seek affirmation from others. I would try *so hard* to be pretty, trendy, and funny. But here's the truth: sometimes people don't think you're pretty, and you have no control over that. I think sometimes Christian messages can feel watered down when we just yell "You're *beautiful!*" Yes, you're beautiful to God, and He created your body just right. But there will always be someone out there who thinks Zach's ex-girlfriend is prettier, and some girl will say your outfit sucks. Sin is ugly and can make you feel ugly. People's opinions differ, and when people don't have the perspective of God's love, they may use your looks to make you feel unworthy. You can't convince everyone you're attractive. But you can know that Christ has called you beautiful from the day He made you.

Plenty of people have thought I wasn't cute. And it sucked. It hurt. But then I woke up the next day and guess what? I was still breathing. Because my purpose isn't to convince people that I'm pretty. God wakes me up each morning to help this world see His beautiful presence.

I want eyes that see my purpose for what it truly is and self-control that reminds me what my purpose is not. I am not a restaurant waiting on a Yelp review or a cake being judged on the Food Network. I am a daughter of Christ.

So brush your hair and wear lipstick if you want, but don't value others' opinions. When someone doesn't choose you, thinks someone is prettier than you, or even says you're ugly—their loss. Turn your heart toward the Lord and away from the opinions of others. Find your worth in your Creator, and love who God made you to be. He meant you for more than people-pleasing.

Dear Jesus, I know that You created me for more than chasing approval from people. Set Your affirmation in my heart so I can let go of others' opinions. Help me have eyes that see my purpose and that don't focus on what I am not. Amen.

16

TO THE GIRL FEELING OVERLOOKED

Then he said to her, "Daughter, your faith
has healed you. Go in peace."

—LUKE 8:48

Whelp . . . there she was . . . Emily.

I was scrolling through Instagram and saw that Emily got a boyfriend. A
cute boyfriend. Also, a pilot boyfriend. Of course she did. Boys were always
paying attention to girls like Emily.

I was in a season of feeling overlooked by my job, every guy on the
planet, my friends, and even my family. As I scrolled, I felt like everyone
but me was getting all the things: the invites, the good grades, the affirmation . . . and a *pilot*.

But while I was feeling forgotten, I was overlooking my Savior's love.

I know you have felt overlooked. It seems like everyone gets more affirmation than you. You watch strangers on TikTok get attention. You stand by
as peers get the prom dates, nice cars, and college acceptances. This feeling
sucks. But it's not from God. He sees you. Stop overlooking your Savior.

The Bible describes a woman who was bleeding for many years. Her
disease was a cultural shame. She was labeled *unclean* and had to stay away

from everyone. When she heard that Jesus was in town, she believed He could heal her. So she ignored the rules of her illness and pushed through the crowd around Jesus. Then she touched His cloak. This woman was shunned and supposed to be hiding, but she went to see Jesus. And amid the pressing crowd, Jesus noticed the touch. He turned to her, healed her, and called her *daughter*.

Her peers told this woman she was unclean and worthless. But her Savior called her *daughter*. Maybe your reputation makes you feel worthless. Maybe the way others ignore you makes you feel boring and overlooked. But your Savior notices you and calls you His.

You may never be the main character of your family, your school, your town. But you are God's daughter. On the days you wonder if your life even matters, reach out to your heavenly Father. Talk to Him. Be honest about your thoughts and anxieties, and ask for healing. Hear Him say, "You weren't called to fit in; you were called to be My daughter."

You'll meet great people in this life, and you'll meet some who overlook you and push you aside. But no human's opinion affects your value. Your worth comes from the Creator. It doesn't matter what the cool kids, cute boy, random mom in your hometown, or strangers think. Push past them and look up. Your Savior is looking at you and calling you *daughter*.

Dear God, may I look to You for my value. I don't need affirmation from others because You call me daughter. Help me remember that You love me not because I caught Your attention but because of Your grace. Amen.

TO THE GIRL STRUGGLING WITH BODY IMAGE

"All people are like grass, and all their glory is like the
flowers of the field; the grass withers and the flowers
fall, but the word of the Lord endures forever."

—1 PETER 1:24–25

If only I had a hotter body . . . he wouldn't have left me.

I thought this lie after a guy kissed me, then left me. A tale as old as time. When I realized he wasn't into me anymore, I started looking at my body as a project that needed to be fixed to be loved. I lost weight, cut my calories, took bikini pictures . . . and still felt worthless. Guys still left me with a broken heart. I also felt overwhelmed and exhausted. I thought abs and a smaller jean size would give me confidence, but the process just caused more pain.

If you're anything like me, body image has been a battle. Social media is full of transformations to compare ourselves to: girls who are now double zeros with six-packs, tight booties, and cute boyfriends, lounging at their beach houses. It's easier than ever to have body-image struggles. You may feel stuck in insecurity. You may have believed the lie that if you could look a certain way, then you would be worth something.

It's normal to struggle with body image, but you don't have to stay in this struggle. Find confidence in your Creator, not in your body. Your body is simply a vessel for your spirit while you're on this earth.

Let me be clear—I'm all for being healthy. Lift those weights, do those squats, eat the brussels sprouts. But always remind yourself to glorify your Creator, not your body. On the days you look in the mirror and feel lies sneak into your brain, remind yourself your body is good. Your legs weren't meant to be hot. God crafted them to take you through the halls, your city, and your travels with joy. Your arms were meant to hug the overlooked, not to be perfectly toned. And your eyes were meant to see God's blessings, not to see others and wish you looked like them. Your body is good because the Creator is good.

No matter how much you work out or diet, your body will betray you in time. It will change shapes; your metabolism will slow down. When we are eighty-five, with gray hair, chilling in rocking chairs, I don't think we'll regret eating that donut. I think we'll see that the Lord's love stands forever.

Our bodies will wither away. But God's Word and your faith will be in your heart forever. Have faith that your Creator made you for a bigger purpose than being "hot."

Dear God, use my legs, arms, stomach, and whole body to glorify You and not myself. Give me the wisdom and discernment to ignore the lies and live confidently in Your truth about my worth. My body isn't a project to be fixed but a gift from You, my Creator. Amen.

18

TO THE GIRL FIGHTING INSECURITY

And over all these virtues put on love, which
binds them all together in perfect unity.

—COLOSSIANS 3:14

After being ghosted by this guy, I saw he posted a picture with a new girl-friend. *Oh, I thought you were Mr. I'm-not-ready-for-anything-serious. Well, you found someone you could be serious for.*

I went to her profile. She was beautiful. Perfect body. No acne. I bet she didn't have an annoying high-pitched voice like me. I bet she was cool. Her clothes were in the latest trend . . .

Then there I was. I had adult acne while she was a doll. I looked like a potato compared to her amazing bikini shot. My insecurity grew while I scrolled her feed.

Comparison only makes us insecure. And insecurity is an ugly battle. Insecurity tells you that others are your competition when they really are your teammates.

Just because she is beautiful does not mean you aren't. And she is probably struggling with insecurity too. The truth is that behind each bikini picture, TikTok star, new girlfriend, and senior picture is a girl who wakes up and doesn't feel pretty enough. According to a Dove study, 96 percent of American women don't label themselves as beautiful. That breaks God's heart.

We struggle with thinking that our worth comes from our appearance—and that is a sin. We are putting the world's view of us ahead of our relationship with Christ. INSECURITY IS CAUSING YOU TO INSULT THE IMAGE OF CHRIST THAT YOU SEE IN THE MIRROR.

This is coming from a girl who spent many of her high school years overdieting and working herself out to the point of crying on the scale. I know insecurity. I know what it feels like to hate your body. But I also know that walking with Christ can save you from those lies. He won't just bibbidi-bobbidi-boo all your insecurities away, but He will walk with you daily. With prayer He will change your perspective from comparison with others to confidence in who He made you to be.

You are worthy and beautiful not because of who you are but because of whose you are. You were created for a reason.

So let's be united with one another instead of trying to compete. We are teammates, not competition. Comparison brings out insecurity; love and unity bring out confidence.

Dear God, I will not let insecurity have the last word on how I view myself. Lord, You knit me together in my mother's womb. You call me beautiful. You did not make a mistake when You created me, and I will celebrate who I am because I know whose I am. Help me live in confidence and unity, not in competition. Amen.

5 THOUGHTS ABOUT YOUR VALUE

1. YOUR LOVE—NOT YOUR APPEARANCE—CHANGES THE WORLD.

2. IT'S A HARD DAY, NOT A BAD LIFE. GOD USES THE HARD THINGS TO LEAD YOU TO HIS GOOD.

3. YOUR FUTURE SELF IS PROUD OF THE YOU RIGHT NOW WHO ISN'T GIVING UP. KEEP PRESSING FORWARD.

4. REJECTION IS PROTECTION. WHEN A DOOR CLOSES, GOD IS DOING SOMETHING NEW AND BEAUTIFUL.

5. NOT EVERYONE WILL SEE YOUR VALUE. BUT YOUR SAVIOR LOVES YOU AND CARES FOR YOU. HE CREATED YOU FOR SOMETHING MORE IMPORTANT THAN PROVING YOURSELF.

Clothe yourself

IN CONFIDENCE OF YOUR CREATOR'S GOODNESS.

And wear the dress you want!

19

TO THE GIRL READY TO FEEL BEAUTIFUL

Therefore, as God's chosen people, holy and
dearly loved, clothe yourselves with compassion,
kindness, humility, gentleness and patience.
—COLOSSIANS 3:12

When I was fifteen, my father took me to a Mardi Gras extravaganza. I grew up near New Orleans, so Mardi Gras was a fun time filled with beads, stuffed animals, and—as you got older—pretty dresses.

My mom took me to the store to get a gown for this Mardi Gras ball. There were so many colorful dresses. I saw a red one with fun fringe on it and loved it. But when I tried it on, I felt fat and ugly. So I decided on a black dress that had a sash. I wish I could say I picked the one I really wanted, but I settled on the black one because I had read on Google that black was slimming.

I had fun at the ball, but I didn't like the way I looked, even in the black dress. Isn't it crazy that no matter how much we diet, what color contact we put in, how much makeup we wear, or how much the dye costs that we put in our hair, we still don't feel pretty? Even though I did everything to feel skinny at that ball—wearing SPANX and all—I still didn't feel good about the way I looked.

See, what I needed wasn't a black dress or shaping underwear. I needed a heart change. I needed eyes that saw myself as made in the image of Christ. I needed the confidence that comes from knowing that my Creator didn't make a mistake on me.

So then there's you. . . . You may have woken up today and searched for a "black dress"—some trick or product to make you prettier. But confidence doesn't come from what we put on. It comes from knowing our Creator.

No one at your funeral will talk about your looks. They will talk about your love. Your legacy is your love. So dress yourself in the characteristics of Christ: compassion, kindness, humility, gentleness, and patience. Clothe yourself in a faith that's confident of your Creator's goodness. And wear the dress you want! Life is about being uniquely you, the girl God created. It's not about being what Google or some boy says is attractive.

Dear God, give me a kind heart and a confident spirit. I know no dress, makeup routine, or product can give me true confidence. Starting today, help me stop trying to live a life that is about being attractive and start living a legacy of love. Amen.

TO THE GIRL APOLOGIZING TOO MUCH

And may you have the power to understand, as all God's
people should, how wide, how long, how high, and how deep
his love is. May you experience the love of Christ, though it is
too great to understand fully. Then you will be made complete
with all the fullness of life and power that comes from God.

—EPHESIANS 3:18–19 NLT

In ninth grade, I wasn't cool. Girls weren't always nice, no guy seemed to ever like me, and I was even asked to homecoming as a joke. It all hurt a lot, and I felt like my presence was a bother to everyone else. So since I felt like a bother, I said sorry a lot. Whenever I said something in a conversation that felt off, I would say sorry. Someone could ask me a question about my day, and somehow, I would say sorry.

That summer, I went to camp and made new friends who made me laugh and were silly with me. They were also kind. Once, we were playing four square and anytime I got someone out, I winced and said, "I'm sorry." After a while, my friend Robyn said, "Grace, you're our friend playing a game with us. There is no need to say sorry." She was being a good friend, something I rarely saw. Her words showed me that my presence didn't need an apology.

I constantly apologized because I thought my life was meaningless. I thought I was annoying. And despite Robyn's words of truth, I continued to struggle with saying sorry as I got older. I remember feeling hurt and worthless after a boy left me. Guess who said sorry? Not him. You could stomp on my heart and still get an apology.

The words *I'm sorry* are important. They need to be said many times. Heartfelt apologies and conviction need to be said. However, you should only apologize for your sin, not for yourself. Don't say words that will allow a lie about your worth to live in your heart.

The Bible tells us to love our neighbors as ourselves (Matthew 22:39). This means we must first love ourselves before we can truly love others. Loving yourself isn't arrogant. We don't love ourselves because we are perfect. We love ourselves because our perfect God made us intentionally. He breathed life into you for a reason.

So on the days you feel like a bother, stop and pray. Love yourself because God first loved you. He didn't create you by accident. Your presence is a gift. Never apologize for it.

Dear God, I have felt like my presence is a bother. Help me love myself because You are a good Creator. Help me live like my presence is something to celebrate, not apologize for. Today, may I find joy in who You created me to be, and may I focus on knowing You more than I focus on being liked. Amen.

TO THE GIRL FEELING PLAIN

For you created my inmost being; you knit me
together in my mother's womb. I praise you
because I am fearfully and wonderfully made; your
works are wonderful, I know that full well.

—PSALM 139:13–14

There is an Instagram filter that I used to be obsessed with. It made my skin look tanner, my hair look brighter, and my teeth appear pearly white. I loved this filter until a guy I was talking to replied to my Instagram story selfie and said, "You look beautiful here!"

Here? Did I not look beautiful in my other pictures? Or worse . . . was I just plain in person?

After this simple interaction, I started getting spray tans regularly and using whitening strips for my teeth. But I still didn't look like those pictures. No amount of makeup or spray tan could make me look like the filter made me look. Because those pictures didn't show *me*. I wasn't plain in person. IN FACT, IN PERSON I WAS BETTER THAN THE PHOTOS—I WAS ME.

In a world where a filter can change how you look to others, please remember that a filter isn't a better version of you. In fact, it's not you at all. I used to depend on filters to feel pretty. And don't get me wrong, I still sometimes may use a filter. But now I see that God created me purposefully and for a purpose. He knit you and me together in our mothers' wombs. He crafted the shape of our eyebrows and sculpted our cheeks to be a little chubby. He created us the way we are for a reason. You don't need a filter. You need eyes that see yourself the way Jesus sees you.

When you take off your makeup, when you're honest about your weird hobby, when you allow yourself to be the *you* that God knit together and created in His image, you find something better than a filtered picture— you find God's beauty in you. The little details about you were handcrafted by the Creator. So don't feel plain. Feel God's perfect fingerprint stamping you to be who you were meant to be.

Dear Creator God, I am not plain. I was uniquely created by You for a purpose. In a culture that tells me I need a filter between myself and the world, remind me that I just need to be the me You crafted. Amen.

TO THE GIRL WANTING TO BE MORE

And now these three remain: faith, hope and
love. But the greatest of these is love.

—1 CORINTHIANS 13:13

I used to want to be more—more beautiful, more toned, more intelligent, more high fashion, and more like the other girls who seemed to get the guys. I never felt that I was enough. I remember one day I was at a birthday dinner for a friend, and everyone walked up in tight dresses and beautiful makeup. I felt like I didn't measure up.

That night I went to bed and tossed and turned. I felt not enough and like I needed to be more. Finally, at 1 a.m., when I still hadn't fallen asleep, I prayed. I prayed and asked God to remove those thoughts and give me peace in who I am. The next morning I ran into an old friend at the gas station. She told me my smile was always beautiful, then walked away. This friend's loving comment made me feel better and made my day.

The truth is that your beauty, your outfit, your trophies, and your grades won't make someone feel better. But your kindness will make people smile. So you and I have a choice: we can choose to be more loving or to waste precious time trying to be more like the world. Have you spent most days trying to be a leader but forgotten to be kind to the new girl? Have you been so focused on being popular that you forgot to be inclusive? Are you trying so hard to be more like someone else because you just never feel enough? Wake up! Your love is more than enough because your love shows others who Christ is.

Showing Christ's love is more important than measuring up to some standard the world decided was a thing. Love isn't about you being more, it's about showing Christ more. Chase your real purpose by making others smile with the love of Christ, which is greatest of all.

Take a deep breath and remember: your accomplishments don't change the world—your love does.

Dear Christ, I often feel like I'm not enough. Please change my perspective and give me confidence in who You made me to be so that I can be more loving instead of focusing on myself. Being loving is the greatest thing I can be. Help me be someone who makes others smile, not someone who is more like the world. Amen.

23

TO THE GIRL FEELING AWKWARD

*Yet you, LORD, are our Father. We are the clay, you
are the potter; we are all the work of your hand.*

—ISAIAH 64:8

I didn't finish losing my baby teeth until I was in high school. In fact, the dentist had to pull those last teeth out so I could get braces. At fifteen, I was missing two teeth in my smile, had braces, and was struggling to master winged eyeliner.

I was awkward. You can try to tell me, "Aw, you were cute." But nope. I was awkward. And the truth is I'm still awkward. I recently tried to use lip liner. My line—well—wasn't a line. My friend had to kindly tell me that my lipstick was going crazy. I once picked my wedgie on a first date. I have the worst dance moves, but I dance anyway. I'm not always good at following the trends; no wonder I'm not a fashion blogger. And I can be kind of cringe. Sometimes I talk too fast or don't say the best thing.

Everyone is afraid of being awkward. BUT THERE'S *NOTHING* WRONG WITH BEING AWKWARD. Being awkward reminds others that we are human. We aren't called to have it all together and be prim and proper. We are called to know the One who uses all things for our good.

One time, there was a new face in my PE class. Her name was Chloe. We sat next to each other, and I awkwardly kept trying to talk to her. I felt weird approaching her, but after a bit I invited her to come to youth group. She came, she accepted Christ, and we became best friends. I was even her bridesmaid eleven years later.

God also used my first breakup for His glory. Two years after I cried to Taylor Swift songs for three weeks over this boy, I was able to comfort a girl crying over her breakup. In college, God used a rumor to help me find my worth in who He says I am and not what others think. God has used my braces, my years of no boys looking my way, my awkward obsession with One Direction, and even my weird hellos to strangers. He is the potter, and I am the clay. The way the Lord designed me was good and brings Him glory.

You're not missing out because you have some awkward tendencies. You're not a bother because you say things that are out of place. God created you, so you are awesome! You can't be cool at all the things, but you can honor God who uses all things.

Dear God, sometimes I feel awkward, but remind me that my awkwardness, cringe habits, and quirkiness aren't hindering me from good. You didn't create me to do all things. You created me to know You, the One who can use all things, including my awkwardness, for Your good. Amen.

24

TO THE GIRL FEELING LIKE A DISAPPOINTMENT

My flesh and my heart may fail, but God is the
strength of my heart and my portion forever.
—PSALM 73:26

One day when my parents picked me up from the airport, I started crying as soon as I jumped in the car. I had just been let go from a job due to budget cuts. I had told my friends that I was scared how my parents would react. My parents are very successful, and sometimes I feel pressure from them to be perfect. I have felt this way since I was young. I remember being obsessed with winning student of the month and other awards to prove myself to them. There was nothing I feared more than being a disappointment.

Maybe you've braced yourself as you shared news with your parents. Or maybe you rush to your room after another lost game, another detention, or another report card to avoid the sideways look. Or perhaps your parent just comes right out and tells you that you're not living up to expectations. That sucks.

Relationships with parents can be hard. They take work and mutual understanding. Parents are messy, sinful humans, and so are we. There were moments my parents made mistakes. There were also moments I was hurtful with my words. And . . . I wrecked two cars in high school. Yeah, I deserved to be yelled at for that.

That day at the airport, my parents were actually really cool. They reminded me that there was more to life than this one job and that I have value because of my Creator, not because of my résumé. But I know I'm lucky to have parents who responded like that.

Here's the truth: even if you feel like a disappointment to your parents, YOU ARE ALWAYS A TREASURED DAUGHTER OF GOD. You feel like a disappointment, but *disappointment* is not your name. Your name is *loved*, *daughter*, and *chosen*. You are His. Don't let a late-night fight or a random criticism cause you to doubt your worth.

Give grace to your parents. If your parents don't love you well, please remember your eternal Father always has open arms for you. He doesn't want your résumé, your perfection, or your win. And He will never pressure you to be something you're not. He loves you, not because of what you do, but because you are His. Take a deep breath and remind yourself that you are amazing. Then remember that an honest conversation and prayer can go a long way in any relationship. But no matter where you're at with your parents, know that you're not a disappointment to God. You are loved.

Dear Jesus, remind me that I'm not a disappointment to You—I am loved. There is nothing I can do to lose Your love. I pray for my relationship with my parents (or guardians). Help me to give them grace. And show them that I need encouragement and grace from them. Amen.

9 REMINDERS FOR THE GIRL READY TO OWN HER WORTH

1. CONFIDENCE COMES FROM KNOWING YOUR CREATOR.

2. GOD KNEW WHAT HE WAS DOING WHEN HE CREATED YOU.

3. YOU'RE WHERE GOD WANTS YOU TO BE.

4. GIVE YOURSELF THE SAME GRACE YOU GIVE OTHERS.

5. YOUR PURPOSE ISN'T TO PROVE THAT YOU'RE WORTH LOVING.

6. CHRIST BELIEVED YOU WERE WORTH DYING FOR.

7. LIES HAVE NO POWER WHERE GOD'S TRUTH LIVES.

8. CLOSE YOUR PHONE AND STOP GETTING DISTRACTED BY OTHERS' BLESSINGS.

9. GOD HAS UNIQUE BLESSINGS FOR YOU.

More
CONTENTMENT

25

TO THE GIRL WHO IS WAITING

Sarah said, "God has brought me laughter, and
everyone who hears about this will laugh with me."

—GENESIS 21:6

The Bible tells us about a woman named Sarah. She was old—sixty-five!—
when angels told her husband that Sarah would give birth to a child and
be the mother of many nations. When she heard about it, she laughed in
disbelief. The angels' promise seemed so impossible that Sarah thought
another woman would have to give birth to Abraham's child for him to
get the promised heir. So she gave her slave to her husband as a wife. But
God told Sarah that was not what He meant. God promised again that the
impossible would happen.

And twenty-five years later, Sarah became pregnant. She gave birth to
a son, even in her *really* old age. And instead of laughing in disbelief, she
laughed in amazement. God transformed her doubt and disbelief into joy.

So there's you. No, you're not ninety expecting a child. But it feels like
you have been waiting for way too long for that peace, friendship, relationship, grade, job, acceptance, family healing, or just a nap. Waiting isn't fun,
but God's blessing is worth it.

And even if you don't get the blessing you are hoping for, you always have a better blessing: the freedom that comes from the blood of Christ. We are free *now* to cry, to dance, to live, and to learn by His side. We are free to be blessed by our Creator and Savior's love. You don't have to wait twenty-five years for this blessing. You can walk through today with the contentment, purpose, joy, sense of adventure, and peace that come from journeying with Jesus.

So instead of being sad about your season of waiting, be expectant. (No, I'm not talking about expecting a six-foot man who loves Jesus and his mama to walk into your life.) Be expectant of God to make a way when it feels like no way is possible. Don't doubt—like Sarah did—that God will bless you. Be expectant of God to speak, even when you feel like He's been silent. God's silence isn't the same as God's absence. He may just be preparing something great for you and through you.

And if you are laughing in doubt, drop your expectations. Stop focusing on what makes sense. It made no sense for Sarah to get pregnant after menopause, but it happened because it was a blessing from God. Focus on your present blessings, and be expectant of what God will do next.

Dear God, I doubt You a lot and laugh at Your promises. Transform my laughter of doubt to laughter of amazement. Remind me that the real blessing is to witness Your miracles and freedom, not a relationship, grade, family, or anything else from this world. Amen.

26

TO THE GIRL WHOSE LIFE
ISN'T GOING HER WAY

I will instruct you and teach you in the way you should
go; I will counsel you with my loving eye on you.

—PSALM 32:8

For a season, college was all fun. I was in the top sorority and the party group. For once, everyone knew my name. But then my life came crashing down. A friend from high school died, then a guy ghosted me. I felt left out of my friend group, and I found out that some girls had a group chat to talk bad about me. Oh, I was also failing my science class.

One minute life feels great, then—*bam!* Everything rushes downhill. So when life feels overwhelming and isn't going our way, how do we respond?

My first reaction used to be anger at God. If God was good, why didn't my life always feel good? I didn't realize that God was using the bad and the twists to refine me. Refining is a process used to make metal stronger. Workers melt the metal in a fire to get out impurities. My hardships, hurt, and change of plans didn't define me; they refined me. They made me stronger! Years later I can see that God was at work. My life wasn't meant to be about my plans. My life isn't about me at all. When I began to let my life be about the Author of love, I found something better than my plans—I found purpose. We get upset about life not going our way because we've taken ownership of what isn't ours.

One time I left a party disappointed. The whole time I had been stuck talking to this new girl. I was hoping to talk to the cute boy I was crushing on, but he didn't say more than a "what's up?" to me. Then that night, I got a text: "Hey Grace! Someone gave me your number. I knew no one tonight and honestly was scared coming to the party. Thanks for talking to me and making me feel welcome." After I got that text, I felt better than I would have if that guy had talked to me. I wasn't missing out; I was living God's purpose at that party.

Your life will not always go your way. But let God show you where to go, then follow Him and not your expectations. Instead of asking why your day or year looked different from what you had hoped, look for God's eye on you. Sometimes the job says no, the cute guy doesn't talk to you, or you don't do well on the test. Sometimes you're just talking to one girl instead of being the life of the party. Life isn't about everything going our way; it's about us going God's way.

Dear Father, life isn't going my way. I'm disappointed, but I know that life isn't about me. Help me find purpose in saying yes to You instead of being attached to the expectations I have for my day and life. I want to go Your way. Amen.

27

TO THE GIRL COUNTING DOWN

This is the day the LORD has made; let's rejoice and be glad in it.

—PSALM 118:24 CSB

In college, I had a countdown on my phone telling the number of days until the next break, whether Christmas break, spring break, or summer vacation. I watched that thing anxiously *every* day and waited for it to tick down. But as the number got smaller, I stressed out more. Because before any break were midterms or finals. Schools always schedule the worst week right when you really need a rest! I would call my mom and say "I hate school!" and stress out in the library. But then when I was home, something always went wrong, and I didn't enjoy the time off.

I thought school was the problem. But when I finally got to sleep in and eat home-cooked food, I still wasn't happy. Each time, my family would fight, or I would run into someone I didn't want to see in my small town, and my negative attitude would grow. As the end of the break neared, I got anxiety about school starting again. Then I was back on campus huffing and puffing to class with my countdown restarted.

Finally, my junior year I thought, *I want to find joy on the Wednesdays.* I prayed to enjoy the in-between and to savor the simple things, like seeing a friend on the way to class or chatting with my coworkers. Slowly, my perspective changed. I realized that my classes were opportunities to have conversations with people who would have been strangers if it wasn't for British Literature or Biology. Slowly, through prayer, I realized God was with me every day (including Wednesdays).

The truth is that joy isn't found in a break or a vacation. Joy isn't found when you catch feelings or catch flights. Joy isn't dependent on your surroundings. That state of calm happiness depends on your perspective. ARE YOU SEEING YOUR BLESSINGS? Do you soak in the sunshine on your way to school? Do you stop to have a conversation when you bump into an old friend? Do you remember that God created this day and created you to be in it?

It's okay to feel tired after a week of deadlines. God is ready to hear your frustrations about the busy Wednesdays, the hard class, and the stress of juggling it all. But even in prayer, don't let negativity stay long. When you find yourself anxious and frustrated, pray for joy. Then look for all the blessings around you. The Creator of sunshine and belly laughs is walking with you. He will bring you things to smile about each day. But you have to step out of the shadow of your negative attitude and look around.

Dear God, the grind has got me feeling tired and frustrated. Help me see Your blessings around me and enjoy each day with You, even during the in-between and busy. Amen.

TO THE GIRL THINKING, *ONE DAY*

You who are young, be happy while you are young, and let your heart give you joy in the days of your youth. Follow the ways of your heart and whatever your eyes see, but know that for all these things God will bring you into judgment.

—ECCLESIASTES 11:9

Where do you see yourself "one day"? I see an attractive man who loves sushi and his mama. I see a cute white house in the suburbs with fresh flowers in my kitchen. I see myself having enough money to get my nails done regularly, maybe with cute designs and all. I see myself chasing big dreams and cute babies.

That's where I hope to be one day, but right now I'm not in that season. I work three jobs and live with roommates. When Trader Joe's flowers are cheap, I'll get them, but that is a treat. And I'm not dating anyone, so there's no wedding in my near future.

I used to idolize my "one day." At first, that seemed like a good thing. I was a hard worker because I always pushed toward my future. But I was making life a ladder, climbing to "one day" instead of enjoying today.

Yes, life has big moments to look forward to, like throwing your graduation cap in the air and meeting new friends on college move-in day. But if you're busy waiting for your next transition or milestone, you're going to miss out on what God is doing in your present.

See, one day you may in fact have children, and they'll ask about your teen and college days. And of course, you'll tell them about your sixteenth birthday bash and graduation and moving out on your own. But when they need comfort or encouragement, those won't be the memories you share. You'll tell them what you did on those random Wednesdays to find joy. You'll tell about walks with friends who are still in your life. You'll share about the hilarious moment at the football game and how you bombed the test after crying in the library and survived to graduate. You'll share how you made an unexpected friend and the teacher's advice that changed your life.

Joy isn't exclusive to big moments. You can find joy today. But if you're just using this day as a stepping stone, you'll miss out on a lot of smiles and meaningful moments. So stop stressing about the future. Live obediently in the present. Your life is beautiful not because of where you will one day be but because of who is next to you today.

Dear Lord, some days are ordinary and stressful. It's easy to feel like I'm just waiting for "one day." Help me drop my expectations for how I want my life to be and instead live in the moment purposefully and obediently. Help me find joy in following Your will in my present, and help me embrace the beauty of this season. Amen.

29

TO THE GIRL TRYING TO COMPETE

For where jealousy and selfish ambition exist, there
will be disorder and every vile practice.

—JAMES 3:16 ESV

A lot of people don't know this about me, but I have an older brother. Everyone calls Edward Joseph "EJ," and growing up, I was often referred to as "EJ's little sister." I used to get jealous of him, and everything turned into a competition. Whenever there was one more Little Debbie or Coca-Cola can, we would hide it from the other. And as we got older, we got competitive about grades, sports, life, leadership, and more. Okay, just kidding. I don't think he cared what I was doing. It was more me just trying to always one-up him. But since he was older, I was always left disappointed. I even started to think my parents liked him more. He did get the bigger bedroom . . .

Comparison is an ugly game. It doesn't allow you to see your talents. You just see what you are not.

Scripture never calls us to be competitive. Don't get me wrong, I hope you work hard, ace your classes, and win your games. But if you're trying to be better than your sibling, friend, or classmate, guess what? You will fail. You may get a better grade or win the game sometimes, but there will always be something they are better at. We each have unique gifts. You are not called to be better than someone else or to win every competition. You are called to be the girl God created you to be.

I tried so long to prove I wasn't just "EJ's little sister." I was *Grace*. But God knew my name the whole time.

So take a deep breath and remind yourself that you aren't called to win—you are called to know your Creator. Why would the sun get jealous of a flower? Both are beautiful, and both are unique. Don't get competitive with people who are meant to be your teammates.

Dear Lord, thank You that You love me and care for me and that You created me to be unique. Help me focus on my abilities and not focus on what others have or can do. Help me love the gifts You gave me and the gifts You have given others. Amen.

30

TO THE GIRL SAYING YES TOO MUCH

The LORD is my shepherd, I lack nothing. He makes me lie down in green pastures, he leads me beside quiet waters, he refreshes my soul. He guides me along the right paths for his name's sake.

—PSALM 23:1-3

I went through a phase when I said yes to everyone and everything. I told myself I had to agree to all the opportunities to get college scholarships, but that wasn't the whole truth. Because of my yes addiction, I often found myself overwhelmed and burned out.

I remember a peer telling me, "Grace, not everyone and everything needs your yes." *What?!* Her words annoyed me, and I didn't listen. Three weeks later while I was studying for a test after getting back from work at midnight, I found myself promising to hang out with friends and to volunteer for a club that weekend. Then I started crying. I was exhausted! My mom heard me panicking and made me go to bed. I failed my test the next day and had to text the girls that I couldn't hang out. I realized I needed a break. And I needed to learn how to say no.

I know it's so annoying when others say "stop saying yes," especially as other people are asking more from you each day. And some things you don't have the option of saying no to. I needed a job in high school in order to afford textbooks in college. I *had* to say yes to my job. But many other things were my choice.

I told myself that I was being helpful. But the truth is that my addiction to yes was an addiction to feeling needed. I tried to meet my desire to feel important with busyness, which only caused exhaustion. LEARNING TO SAY NO WAS ABOUT LEARNING TO BE CONTENT WITH OTHERS NOT NEEDING ME. Sometimes I had to let the show go on and enjoy the fun party from social media.

Contentment isn't just about embracing life when it doesn't go your way. It also means accepting that you are human. You can only do so much. And when you say yes without asking God for discernment about His will for you, you are glorifying yourself and not God. Contentment is realizing that when you walk with Jesus, you lack nothing. You'll miss out on some things. But you will have the energy and time to do the purposeful things that God sets before you. When you carefully choose when to say yes and when to say no, you will have the contentment that comes from following God down the right path for *you*. That path will glorify Him and bring you true blessings.

Dear God, give me the discernment to know when something is Your will and when saying yes would be acting out of a sinful desire to feel needed. Help me seek Your purpose for me and create healthy boundaries. Amen.

TO THE GIRL NOT RESTING

The LORD replied, "My Presence will go
with you, and I will give you rest."

—EXODUS 33:14

My college sophomore year I was addicted to Diet Coke. I had multiple a day and even sometimes drank one at night. But when I drank one past 7 p.m., I struggled to go to sleep. As I tossed and turned, I would think about all the things I had to do. Then the next day, I would down Diet Coke to give me the energy I needed to get through my to-do list. Finally, I started to cut out Diet Coke, and I made sure to not have it after 5 p.m. Slowly, it became easier to sleep. All it took for me to get the sleep I needed was one simple change to what I was putting in my body. I love Diet Coke, but it isn't my friend when it comes to getting rest.

Sometimes the things we think we enjoy or need keep us from better things. What we put in our days, our bodies, and our minds either helps or hurts our rest and contentment. If you're on social media 24/7, you will also probably be insecure. If you're opening up your school or work email late at night, you will likely be anxious at bedtime. If you're waiting until the last minute to study, you will be stressed and exhausted when you give up and go to bed.

But if you add a prayer, a walk without your phone, a call to a friend who points you to Jesus, or time reading a devotional like this one, your heart will have room to rest. Rest isn't just a nap or lying on a fancy beach, and it isn't only a luxury of the wealthy. Rest is something Christ offers each of us, no matter our situation. Rest is knowing your Creator, finding contentment in who He is, and not worrying about what you can't be.

Think about your daily and weekly routines. Where does your time go? What do you count on to get through the week? What do you do in your downtime? Ask God to help you be honest about whether your habits are helping you create times of rest or keeping you from the peace of contentment in Christ. What can you change to help you focus on God and listen for His guidance? Can you find time to pray while driving to school or while stretching before practice? Can you add a walk with a worship song or talk to a mentor about your friend group? Add rhythms of rest, and remove anything that stops you from being able to find true rest.

Dear God, show me the things in my life that keep me from rest. Help me add rhythms into my life that remind me who You are and help me be content in who You created me to be. I am not called to hustle; I am called to know You. I know that contentment in You is enough, and I will seek Your peace each day. Amen.

4 TRUTHS FOR THE GIRL
CONSTANTLY HUSTLING

1. YOU CAN'T DO EVERYTHING. SAY NO TO THINGS THAT AREN'T LEADING YOU TO THE FUTURE YOU DESIRE.

2. REST ISN'T SOMETHING YOU EARN. REST IS A RHYTHM YOU NEED TO SCHEDULE.

3. YOUR FAVORITE SHOW WON'T GIVE YOU REST. TRUE REST COMES FROM SLOWING DOWN, TAKING A DEEP BREATH, AND REMEMBERING GOD IS IN CONTROL.

4. YOUR LOVE IMPACTS THE WORLD, NOT YOUR SUCCESS. DON'T BE TOO BUSY TO BE LOVE.

32

TO THE GIRL WHO HAS FAILED

*The righteous may fall seven times but still get
up, but the wicked will stumble into trouble.*
—PROVERBS 24:16 CEB

There's a scar under my chin from when I got my first bike. It was Christmas Day, and I was seven years old. I was finally ready for my big-girl bike, and Santa brought me a shiny pink one. I wanted to ride it immediately, so my dad took me outside, and I pedaled as fast as I could. I started going too fast and busted my chin open. A neighbor who was a doctor gave me stitches in his garage, and I remember crying in pain.

On my right thigh, there's another scar. When I was sixteen, I signed up to learn mountain biking at camp. I was so scared to take this skill because it was hard. I thought about switching out for crafts, but I knew that I wanted to ride a bike in the mountains that summer. Well, on one of the first rides, I fell and cut my leg. The wound hurt, and the nurse asked me if I wanted to switch out of the class. But I quickly said no. After that fall, I got back up on the bike with my upper thigh wrapped in a bandage. And I became obsessed with mountain biking.

Now I can see two scars that came from two different biking falls, but

I'm thankful. The falls made me a better biker, and I didn't allow either of those failures to be the final chapter in my biking journey. I actually ended up teaching young girls mountain biking at that camp for many summers. What started as failure turned into opportunity. I helped the girls when they fell, and I got to show them that you can always get back up.

Here's the truth: you are going to fail. You are a flawed human, and you will fall off your bike, make a mistake, bomb a homework assignment, not make the team, and send an email with an embarrassing typo. But what will you do after? Are you going to get back up? When you see a girl going through a breakup, struggling in school, or questioning her purpose, will you teach her that she can keep going?

You may have emotional scars that sting. Some scars never go away, like the scars on my chin and thigh and a few more on my heart. But press on with trust that each scar is a story you can tell later to pull someone else back up. Yes, it's a story of your failure but also of God's strength. Get back up and trust that your failure today is God's opportunity tomorrow.

Dear Jesus, thank You for helping me when I fall. Remind me that my failure today is Your opportunity tomorrow. Use my scars to be a testament of what You've done. I know that failure is certain, but Your strength is also guaranteed to those who call out to You. Amen.

TO THE GIRL STUCK IN HER FEELINGS

*If our hearts condemn us, we know that God is greater
than our hearts, and he knows everything.*

—1 JOHN 3:20

Did you know that your feelings can lie to you? Like when I didn't get a homecoming date, and I cried because I was obviously the least popular girl in school. Or like when I practiced for days and still didn't make the dance team. I was so disappointed and thought I had zero talents. In each of these situations, I spent days sobbing, sitting in my emotions longer than I should have.

Other times, however, I pushed my feelings away until I blew up. After being bullied by my "friends" in middle school, I went home and yelled at my parents for no reason. I would get stressed with school, then be mean to my brother and fall apart if the grade wasn't what I wanted. When I went through a breakup, I avoided the pain by eating junk food late at night. Bottling up your feelings and pushing them away only ends badly.

See, having feelings isn't bad. It's important to feel, mourn, and give yourself the grace to express your thoughts. You should never avoid your hurt or your feelings. However, you also shouldn't stay in your feelings.

And you shouldn't rely on them for truth. When we are surrounded by our hurt, we can't see past it to God's goodness. Sitting in the negative emotions of our present situation means we aren't looking forward to find hope. But when we take a break from the feelings to notice all our blessings and remember what God says, we can find contentment. CONTENTMENT SAYS THAT EVEN WHEN LIFE DOESN'T GO EXACTLY HOW WE WANT, GOD'S GOODNESS IS BIGGER THAN OUR FEELINGS. When we fix our eyes on Him, we find hope, comfort, and the strength to deal.

So today, whether you're upset about a test grade, a friendship that went south, an ex-boyfriend who left you confused, or a team you didn't make . . . remember to feel, then deal. Feel the feelings, then ask God to help you deal with them. Jesus is the only comfort in times of hardship. Only Jesus can give you hope in the middle of eating ice cream on a hard day. I mean, the ice cream does help, but Jesus provides true comfort as well as a path back to hope.

Your feelings aren't anything to avoid, but they aren't truth you can build a foundation on. Find truth in who Christ is, and don't trust your feelings. Recognize the hurt, disappointment, and overwhelm you feel, but then release your burden to Christ and seek the truth from Him.

Dear God, help me to feel, then deal. Remind me that while my feelings aren't bad, contentment comes from acknowledging how I feel and then leaning on You for comfort and truth. Thank You that You are with me, even when I'm in my feelings. Amen.

34

TO THE GIRL STUCK IN HER PAST

"Forget the former things; do not dwell on the past. See, I am doing a new thing! Now it springs up; do you not perceive it? I am making a way in the wilderness and streams in the wasteland."

—ISAIAH 43:18–19

As I scrolled Instagram one day, one video made me stop. Jacob had gotten married. Jacob was a boy I had a fling with, and then I walked away for dumb reasons. He was a good guy who loved Jesus. And if I'm being honest, I wasn't mature enough to recognize a good thing. And now there he was, marrying a very cute girl in a trendy wedding dress with fun sleeves. I bet his mom was so excited. Love looked amazing on him.

After seeing Jacob's wedding photos in my feed, I got mad at myself. Why didn't I date Jacob? I had missed out on a good man because I wasn't mature enough, and now this pretty girl was going to have a great life with him instead of me. Next, I started looking back on other things from my past. What else had I done that caused me to miss out? It didn't take long for me to lose contentment in my current season.

Here's the truth: if you look back on your past choices for too long, you'll miss out on your present blessings. You can't change your past, but you can have hope for your future. God is always doing something new and making a way, even when there seems to be no way. **YOUR PAST DOESN'T HAVE AS MUCH POWER OVER YOUR FUTURE AS JESUS DOES.**

Sometimes we deny a good guy, party too much, kiss the wrong boys, stay too quiet, or don't join that club. Learn from the past, but don't obsess over it. Look forward with hope and expectation at what God will do in your life. You can't change the past, but you can walk forward in the belief that God is making a way. Scripture says God will make a way even if you are in a wilderness of life. In the wilderness, life isn't easy. There are hardships around you, and it's easy to feel alone. But God can bring life into the wasteland. He will bring you good things that are as refreshing as cold water in the desert. When you feel like you missed out and your past has left no room for hope in your future, remember that God always makes a way. Look forward toward His special path for you.

Dear God, I regret things I did in my past. But I know that the hope I have in You is more powerful than any past decision I've made. Help me to look forward and see the new thing You are doing. Thank You for always making a way, even when it feels like I've wandered into a wilderness in my life. Amen.

35

TO THE GIRL READY TO MOVE ON

Wait for the LORD; be strong and take
heart and wait for the LORD.

—PSALM 27:14

When I drove off to college, I was ready to move on from high school and my small town. Each morning of my senior year, I told my mom, "I can't wait to graduate." Even in eighth grade I had a countdown to graduation . . . from high school.

I think a lot of us have felt ready to move on long before a season is over. Maybe you are ready to move on from this school year or school in general. Maybe you are ready to find a job that pays better and where the boss actually knows your name. Maybe you want to go to that next big city or forget the drama from last semester. I know how you feel, but stop and look around. God led you to this present moment for a purpose. Your location is purposeful, and your daily tasks are opportunities.

In the Bible, we read about Moses, whose life was a wild ride. Born when the Israelites were slaves in Egypt, he was almost murdered as a baby and then was adopted by a princess. When Moses got older, God spoke to him and called him to help the Israelites escape Egypt. God told Moses that He would bring the people out of Egypt, but first Moses needed to give Pharoah God's messages.

Let me be honest here. If I were Moses, I would have been frustrated by God's give-it-a-second plan. The Israelites were in slavery . . . and God wanted to give messages to the king oppressing them before they could escape? I would have told God something like, "Let's do this! If You're going to free us, why wait?" But God had a plan. Moses repeated God's message to Pharoah to let the people go. And as Pharoah continued to refuse, God brought nasty plagues of frogs, gnats, and bloody water. God showed His power through Moses, and all the countries around Egypt heard about it. So when the Israelites finally escaped, the other nations were afraid to mess with them. God's "slow" plan protected them.

So yes, you want to move on. Maybe you feel like Moses, and God is taking longer than you expected. It's easy to want to rush God's plan. We often think we know better, and if He could or would just fix things, then life would finally be better. But God isn't trying to hinder anything good from your life. He cares for you and is leading you to protection. Trust Him, even when His timing feels weird or slow.

Dear God, there are things in my life I want to move on from, but I know You have a purpose for me right now. Help me find You in the journey and see the opportunities You are giving me. Help me work for Your purpose, even in the moments of life I try to rush. Remind me that the present is beautiful because You are here with me working out Your plans. Amen.

36

TO THE GIRL THINKING,

WHEN I'M OLDER

But the LORD said to me, "Do not say, 'I am too young.'
You must go to everyone I send you to and say whatever
I command you. Do not be afraid of them, for I am
with you and will rescue you," declares the LORD.

—JEREMIAH 1:7–8

As a college freshman, I had a plan for the kind of woman I would become. She would be a boss but would also know how to make a mean apple pie. She would wear classy midi dresses and have her life together. Oh, and she would do cool things for Jesus. I envisioned a modern, classy, Sunday-school-teaching thirty-year-old, and I thought she would be all that God wanted me to be. She would be bold in faith and not afraid to speak up.

But at that time, I wasn't living for God. I wanted to find purpose . . . one day. But while I was a freshman, I thought I was supposed to be young, wild, and free. I thought that meant going a little crazy, finding myself, and learning lessons the hard way. One day I would figure it out and find God, but that could wait until I was older. However, I soon learned that the party lifestyle, the insecurity, the comparison, and the struggle of trying to run away from God was not freeing. I was miserable, and I felt trapped by the image I was trying to live up to.

What I really needed was confidence in who I was at *that* time, not just hope about who I could be. God didn't want this midi-dress-wearing future me who cooked apple pie and had life figured out. God wanted me—the nineteen-year-old college freshman, the sorority hopeful, the messy room-mate. I only started to feel free when I realized that God could use my youth, and I began living for Him.

YOUR AGE DOESN'T DISQUALIFY YOU FROM SERVING GOD. You may feel like you don't have life figured out. But the truth is that no matter how old you are, you won't "figure life out." Life is hard and confusing and always changing. The important thing to figure out is that God wants you, loves you, and gives you true freedom. Chasing God's purpose for you is more wild and more freeing than anything the high school or college "experience" offers. Be carefree in your walk with Christ, not careless in your youth. Free yourself from worries about what others think or what you may miss out on. You can do amazing things for God right now. Don't waste the potential for purpose *now*. Run toward the true freedom of life with Christ.

Dear God, thank You for showing me that my age isn't anything to waste. I pray to be carefree in my love for You, not careless in my walk with You. I know that freedom comes from You, not from wasting away my younger years. Amen.

37

TO THE GIRL STILL FIGURING IT OUT

I know what it is to be in need, and I know what it is
to have plenty. I have learned the secret of being
content in any and every situation, whether well fed
or hungry, whether living in plenty or in want. I can
do all this through him who gives me strength.

—PHILIPPIANS 4:12–13

When I spoke at high school graduation, a lot of people complimented me. But many also saw that when I was supposed to start the Pledge of Allegiance before my speech, I was so nervous that I said it at the wrong time. My principal literally whispered, "Get it together, Grace."

One time at a book signing, a girl praised me for having my life together because I was an author at a young age. What she didn't know was that I wasn't making enough money off my book, and I would do any job to make side cash. During this time I was actually doing laundry for a nice lady to help pay my bills.

Another time a friend asked me how I stayed confident in being single. I laughed and told her, "I'll let you know when I figure it out."

I don't have it all figured out, and chances are that neither do you.

We are both living and learning. But we aren't called to have all our stuff together; we are called to know the One who can use all things and all situations for good. You are not a hot mess, you are a holy mess, and God can use you wherever you are.

Does this season of your life feel like an experiment or like a journey through an uncharted wilderness? It's okay to be in a time of trying things, making mistakes, and learning. Enjoy the process and stop "faking it till you make it." You don't need to have all the answers. Don't get frustrated if your life isn't where you thought it would be by now. Maybe you know exactly what your career will be. Or maybe you're taking classes to see what you like. Maybe you have plenty of options for jobs and internships, or maybe you're hungry for good friends. We don't have to have it all figured out to experience contentment. All you need is Christ, who will strengthen you to do all the things He desires for you.

Dear God, I don't have it all figured out. Sometimes I feel like I have plenty of knowledge, but other times I feel like I am living without a clue. Remind me that even when I don't have it figured out, You have wisdom and goodness. Help me be content in Your strength and not feel frustrated by my learning process. Amen.

TO THE GIRL WANTING MORE THINGS

Keep your lives free from the love of money and be
content with what you have, because God has said,
"Never will I leave you; never will I forsake you."

—HEBREWS 13:5

If only I had this blow-dryer . . . then my hair would finally look good!

A couple of years ago, I saw all these influencers use this popular Dyson blow-dryer. And then I was in a wedding as a bridesmaid and one of the other bridesmaids had this fancy blow-dryer too. Of course, her hair was fabulous. I used her blow-dryer, and I loved it. I just had to have it!

But when I found the blow-dryer online, I realized it cost over $500. Was this blow-dryer made of diamonds? Did it spew out crystals, perfume, and happiness? Would it make my hair look like Marilyn Monroe's? Those were the only excuses I could think of for it being $500.

I knew I could not afford a $500 blow-dryer. But then I kept seeing it. Scrolling TikTok, I saw all these cute bloggers with great hair posting about it. Now I was sad I didn't have the blow-dryer, jealous of these Texas bloggers with big hair and big budgets, and disappointed that I was missing out on a chance to be pretty.

I decided to save up my money for this must-have fancy blow-dryer. Months later, I finally had it in my online shopping cart and was entering my payment info. But I suddenly felt uneasy.

I realized that I wasn't buying the blow-dryer because I wanted a good blow-dryer. I was buying this blow-dryer because I thought I needed this new thing to be happy. And I had started to think of how I could get more money to buy more nice products to make me prettier because pretty people are happier . . . right? But I didn't need more beauty tools or even more money. I needed more contentment.

CONTENTMENT MEANS YOU ARE CONFIDENT IN WHO YOU ARE AND OKAY WITH WHO YOU ARE NOT. I am not someone who has a ton of cash or a fancy blow-dryer, but that's okay. I'm not missing out. My God has given me the treasure of His presence. I find contentment when I have confidence in who my Creator is and the simple, sometimes messy, but beautiful life He has given me.

So remind yourself that it is okay to want things, but you don't need things to be happy. You don't need more money or a fancy blow-dryer. You need God, and you already have Him. He will never leave you.

Dear God, thank You for giving me my imperfect but beautiful life. Help me be content with what I have and with who You are. You are more than enough for me. Remind me to be confident in who I am and okay with who I am not. Amen.

5 REMINDERS FOR THE GIRL
READY TO BE CONTENT

1. BE CONFIDENT IN WHO YOU ARE AND OKAY WITH WHO YOU ARE NOT.

2. YOU DON'T NEED ALL THE THINGS; YOU NEED THE ONE WHO CAN USE ALL THINGS FOR GOOD.

3. GOD IS WRITING YOUR STORY. YOUR LIFE WON'T GO EXACTLY HOW YOU WANT, BUT IT IS BEING WRITTEN BY A GOOD AUTHOR.

4. SOMEONE IS PRAYING FOR SOMETHING THAT YOU HAVE RIGHT NOW.

5. YOU HAVE SOMETHING NOW THAT YOU ONCE PRAYED FOR. THANK GOD FOR WHAT HE HAS ALREADY GIVEN YOU.

39

TO THE GIRL FEELING HURT

Bear with each other and forgive one another if any of you has
a grievance against someone. Forgive as the Lord forgave you.

—COLOSSIANS 3:13

For years I was the girl at the end of the lunch table. Don't act like you don't know what I'm talking about. We all know that the cool girls in high school sit in the center seats, like they're royalty. Girls like me are edge-seat girls—always on the brink of being pushed out, removed, and not included.

Being an edge-seat girl was hard, and there were many times when I felt left out. But one experience was especially difficult. I found out a lot of my friends were talking bad about me. They started a horrible rumor, and I was hurt. For *years* this betrayal stayed in my head. Six years later, one of the mean girls started selling makeup, and guess what? I bought some. I still wanted her to like me, but I also craved an apology. No matter how many lip glosses I bought, she never apologized.

You have been hurt. And you may never get the apology you deserve. But here's the truth: when you live a loving life, you sacrifice having a fair life. There will be plenty of times you are the more loving one and plenty of times you are the better friend. There will be people who walk on you, and there will be apologies you never receive.

You don't owe anyone trust, but you do owe your Savior love. And when you love Jesus, you'll realize those who hurt you are also loved by your good God. He will give you the discernment to not trust them but also the boldness to love them and forgive them. Don't hang around waiting on an apology. Get busy living a life of love. Love isn't fair, but love is life changing.

I'm sorry that friend, that boy, that teacher hurt you. I'm sorry they haven't apologized. But look up. Your Savior is working in your hard times. He's giving you the boldness to love those who have hurt you. So on the days the scar stings and you see her profile and wonder if she even thinks about you, look to your Savior as your example. He loved even the people who hung Him on the cross. His best friend Peter denied knowing Him three times when Jesus was arrested. But Jesus forgave him, and Peter became one of the first evangelists to tell others about Jesus. Your Savior loves you despite your messy heart. And your Savior wants you to give grace to others and their messes—not for their gain, but for your peace. Be kind, but not so they will apologize. Be kind and forgive because that's what Jesus did for you.

Dear God, I feel hurt. But I know that living a kind life is more important than living a fair life. Thank You for forgiving me. Change my heart so that I can love and forgive others. Amen.

TO THE GIRL NOT INVITED

As you come to him, the living Stone—rejected
by humans but chosen by God and precious to
him—you also, like living stones, are being built
into a spiritual house to be a holy priesthood.

—1 PETER 2:4-5

Have you ever gotten onto social media and realized there was a party you weren't invited to? Worst feeling, right?

When I was sixteen, I asked some of my friends to go shopping with me Friday after school. Each one had an excuse. One had her grandma in town, one wasn't feeling great, and another was having a family dinner. But then I opened Snapchat that night and saw them all together . . . shopping. I cried. Then I started wondering . . .

Am I annoying?
Am I just not cool enough?
Maybe they thought my joke was stupid the other day.
Maybe they're embarrassed to hang out with me.

It sounds dramatic now, but feeling like you aren't wanted or liked hurts. Being left out can cause your mind to spiral. But the truth is, your life is meant for more than an invitation to a party, a team, or a certain lunch table. You have more important things to do.

Chances are that you, too, know the sting of rejection. Here's the truth: you won't always be invited, and you won't always be wanted. You are lonely now, but *lonely* isn't your name. God calls you *loved, daughter,* and *friend.* You have an invitation to His love. His love isn't exclusive. His love isn't dependent on what you look like or whether you're in student government. It's a gift you are invited to open anytime.

We can't always be the most popular girls in the room, and I don't think God wants us to be. BUT WE CAN BE THE KIND ONES. I can be the one who has felt lonely and so goes out of my way to do life with my arms open, embracing everyone. The sting of being left out is real. It hurts. But let the love and the invitation from your Savior be more powerful than the rejection from your peers. When you aren't invited, remember that your God goes with you in all your seasons. He's there on the Friday night you feel alone, and He's there on the Monday morning you try to make a new friend. Accept His invitation to be loved, and live out this love.

Dear heavenly Father, my loneliness hurts, and I feel rejected. But I know You are always with me. You put me on this earth for a bigger purpose than being in demand. Remind me to be the person who lives out Your love and invites people into Your love. Amen.

TO THE GIRL WITH CHANGING FRIENDSHIPS

"He changes times and seasons; he removes kings
and sets up kings; he gives wisdom to the wise and
knowledge to those who have understanding."

—DANIEL 2:21 ESV

When I went to a college nine hours away, I tried to keep up with my high school friendships. But my new life at school and the new sea of people there naturally took my attention. I focused on my classes, my new friendships, my part-time job, and my sorority. The time spent apart created a distance between my high school friends and me. We changed and grew.

Some people are only in your life for a season. That doesn't mean the friendship or relationship ended horribly. It doesn't mean you have to resent someone who is no longer present in your life. It just means you're growing.

To walk purposefully in your present, you have to look forward. If you keep looking back and wishing things had happened differently, you won't be able to see God's blessings for your future.

You've outgrown those jeans from freshman year of high school, and you've also outgrown some friends from your past. Seasons end. And they don't end because there's bad blood; you simply can't carry everything into your new season. Be thankful for the people who made you who you are. But don't be sad that things are different. Different is a part of growth. Be thankful for the impact someone had on your life. You're allowed to outgrow some friendships, you're allowed to create boundaries, and you're allowed to move on. Move on with gratitude.

Our God uses both the past and present to help us grow. So today is the perfect day to look back on the childhood friends, family members who passed, even old teachers and hard classes, and see that God used these experiences to prepare you for future opportunities while also using the old to make you stronger.

Miley Cyrus released a song in 2008 called "The Climb." This song got me through eighth grade! And the lyrics are true; life is a climb. You see certain views in certain seasons and not in others. Sometimes to go forward, you have to walk away from something. That's okay. God is doing something new.

Dear God, thank You for always working for my good. I pray for trust and faith in Your ability to use my past seasons for Your good in my present and future seasons. Amen.

TO THE GIRL WONDERING IF SHE'LL EVER FIND HER PEOPLE

Two are better than one, because they have a good return for their labor: If either of them falls down, one can help the other up. But pity anyone who falls and has no one to help them up.... A cord of three strands is not quickly broken.

—ECCLESIASTES 4:9–10, 12

I drove away from high school on my last day thinking, *Well, that was it.*

Four years earlier, I had gone to an orientation for eighth graders. I had walked the high school's halls nervous, excited, and thinking, *Surely in a school this big, I will find my people.* But there I was, done with high school and feeling the same sense of loneliness.

Most high school seniors spend their last summer before college at home so they can say goodbye to their friends. But I decided to spend my summer working at a camp as a junior counselor. As I drove eight hours to North Carolina, I prayed, *Lord, let me find the women who will be my bridesmaids one day. Lord, help me find my people.*

And I did! At camp that summer and that year in college, I found amazing friends. Sometimes we think God isn't listening, but He's just preparing our blessings.

Young Christian women are often told to pray for their future husbands, and that is a wonderful thing. However, we should also pray for our future bridesmaids—those special friends we'll want beside us on one of the most important days of our lives.

If you don't have quality friendships, don't panic—you are not alone. But be bold enough to pray for Christian friends and trust that God has good people out there for you.

You crave friendship because friendship is good. Friendship is a gift from God. When you hang out with friends who love well, this is called *fellowship*. God loves fellowship. Actually, God *is* fellowship. He is the Trinity: Father, Son, and Spirit all hanging out as One. YOU LONG FOR FRIENDS BECAUSE YOU ARE MADE IN GOD'S IMAGE. Celebrate your God-given desire for relationships, and trust that He is listening.

If this season feels lonely, love big and wait on the Lord. Pray for friends, and don't be afraid to ask people to hang. If you have your people, pray for them and remind yourself you are better with others. Pray for your bridesmaids.

Dear God, some days I wonder if I'll ever find my people. Grow the friendships I have, and send me good people who will love me well. I pray for those who will be my bridesmaids one day. Help me trust that Your blessings are coming and there is purpose in my current season. Amen.

TO THE GIRL FEELING LIKE
THE SECOND CHOICE

But you are a chosen race, a royal priesthood, a holy
nation, a people for his own possession, that you
may proclaim the excellencies of him who called
you out of darkness into his marvelous light.

—1 PETER 2:9 ESV

I was talking to this guy, and I thought he liked me a lot. Then I heard rumors that he was still talking to his ex. Then he left me for the ex. Classic.

But then of course he and the ex didn't work out—because usually if you break up once, you'll break up again. After he and the ex broke up the second time, he came back to me. I tried to like him again, but my head kept reminding me, *You were his second choice.*

One of his friends said, "You weren't really his second choice, he just needed to find closure." I wanted to believe that. But deep down I knew that if his hot, brunette, tan ex texted him, he would leave me again. He liked this other girl more than me, no doubt.

There's a country song I love called "Jolene." Dolly Parton begs a girl not to take her man because Dolly knows the girl could have him if she wanted to. This is how I feel a lot of times. I feel like the second choice to every other girl: the backup job candidate, the forgotten friend, the homecoming date who was still available. And there are plenty of Jolenes out there who get picked first and are always wanted.

But that's okay.

You might be one guy's, one job's, or one friend's second choice. But your purpose on this earth isn't to be the top dog or everyone's first draft pick. Your purpose is to be loving. And love has a name: Jesus.

When Jesus hung on the cross that dreary day, He chose to die for you. You weren't His afterthought. And each day, despite your mess, your wrinkled dress, botched audition, rejection, or bad grade, Jesus chooses to stay beside you.

God has set you apart from this world as His. It sounds dramatic, but it's true. Because you are God's chosen daughter, this dark world will reject you. But being God's child also means that God has chosen you to be His light in the world. He gives you His light of love and purpose and calls you to share it with others. You may be someone's second choice, but you are Jesus' chosen child. There is no Jolene when it comes to Christ's love. No one can steal His love and light.

Dear God, thank You for choosing me. Take away my insecurity and remind me that my purpose is bigger than being someone's first choice. My purpose is to love and tell others that love has a name. I believe You are love, God. Amen.

44

TO THE GIRL BEING THE BETTER FRIEND

Love is patient, love is kind. It does not envy, it does not boast,
it is not proud. It does not dishonor others, it is not self-
seeking, it is not easily angered, it keeps no record of wrongs.

—1 CORINTHIANS 13:4–5

"I feel like I'm always the better friend when it comes to Kaley," I said to a mentor one day.

I was the friend always remembering to hang out. I was the friend who always cared to FaceTime. I was the friend ready to be there at a moment's notice. I was the friend always reminding her that she was worthy and listening to her problems.

My mentor replied, "Love keeps no records of wrongs." I was annoyed by this response. Wasn't it fair for me to want a friendship that was fifty-fifty?

But the truth was that I became friends with Kaley when she was going through a breakup and experiencing heartache, hurt, and loneliness. She really needed me in that season. But shortly after I called myself the better friend, I had another friend betray me. I'll never forget that Kaley drove three hours to see me. She bought me dinner and listened to my emotions.

See, friendships aren't fifty-fifty. Living a purposeful life isn't always fair. While it is important to have friends who choose you and are there for you, living in grace means forfeiting fairness. Instead of seeking the fairness of fifty-fifty, seek to live a loving life. Love does not keep a record of wrongs, of unanswered FaceTimes, or of someone's availability to hang out. Love gives grace. Sometimes your friends will need you to care for them. Sometimes they will only be able to contribute 30 percent of the relationship. Instead of keeping score, love them.

Jesus is a friend to all, and He calls His followers to befriend everyone. You don't have to be everyone's best friend—that would be impossible. But give love to those who need it. Love doesn't expect anything in return. So stop thinking about being a "better" friend and start realizing that God is giving you opportunities to live out His purpose. Offer love without keeping a record.

Dear Father, I am thankful that You are a friend to all. Help me to not hold a record or focus on being a favorite friend or first choice but to live a loving and purposeful life. Help me look after my friends who are hurting and accept help from friends in my time of need. Amen.

45

TO THE GIRL HATING
THE SINGLE LIFE

*Trust in the LORD with all your heart and lean not
on your own understanding; in all your ways submit
to him, and he will make your paths straight.*
—PROVERBS 3:5-6

I recently found a tweet of mine from 2014. When I wrote it, I was a senior in high school. I was also way too invested in *The Bachelor*. (Funny how things don't change!) I tweeted that if I was still single at twenty-five, I would go on *The Bachelor*. Well, here I am.

Many of us have this mindset about singleness. We decide that we want to be married by a certain age and have kids before another age. Without realizing it, we have tried to be the authors of our lives. I used to think like this. I used to struggle with being single. But lately I've been trusting God to write my story.

You are not pathetic for wanting a relationship. It's tough to not go there when your friends have boyfriends. Or when you've gone through a breakup. Or if you're feeling like guys don't even give you a chance. Whatever your singleness situation, it isn't a sin to want a boyfriend. But when you focus on what you don't have or make ultimatums, you miss out on the peace that comes from letting God be God.

You don't need another person to tell you, "It happens when you least expect it." So many people say that. (I know this personally!) You also don't need to hear, "You will definitely get married." Marriage isn't promised. You need to hear that God is a good Author. If you could see the big picture that He sees, you would understand the purpose in your singleness.

You can be single and desire marriage. BUT CHOOSE TO SEE THE GOOD IN YOUR TODAY. There are *so* many benefits to being on your own. Spend the entire weekend at your best friend's house. Be an athlete without worrying about stepping on some guy's macho toes. Study abroad! You don't have to struggle. Struggling means you're trying to get out of it and aren't comfortable as you. You should always feel comfortable when you're walking with your heavenly Father.

God hasn't failed you because He didn't give you a six-foot prom date who loves Mexican food. It won't mean that He's failed you if you're still single at twenty-six. Your God is writing your story, and the plot is about something greater than finding a boy. God's story for you is about finding purpose. If you're too busy looking around for a guy to complete you, you'll miss out on the contentment that comes from living on purpose and trusting God.

Dear heavenly Father, help me find purpose and contentment in the story You are writing for me. I know that no relationship with a human can make me more valuable. Your relationship with me is what matters most. Amen.

46

TO THE GIRL TRYING TO BE EVERYONE'S FRIEND

A friend loves at all times.

—PROVERBS 17:17

In high school, I always felt left out and lonely. So when I went to college, I told myself I would have a lot of best friends. I hung out with everyone. At one point, one of my many best friends was struggling with her boyfriend and broke up with him. She told me about the split, but because I was juggling so many friendships, I forgot. When I saw her the next time, I asked where her ex was. I said the worst thing!

My heart wasn't in a bad place with trying to be everyone's best friend. I thought I was being loving. As the Christian girl, I thought I was *supposed* to be everyone's best friend. However, I realized that was impossible. I was exhausted from trying to spend time with everyone, listen to everyone, and help everyone. And even though I know better now, I still try to do too much with friendships sometimes. I desperately want *everyone* to like me, and I desire many friendships. But I've learned that it is more important to know a few people well than to know a lot of people's names. How sad would it be if a good friend of yours was struggling with her parents, boyfriend, or insecurity, and you forgot to ask about her heart because you were too busy?

Let me be clear: Jesus wants you to love everyone. But that doesn't mean you have to commit yourself to everyone. You can be kind to everyone. You can take time to meet a need for a classmate or neighbor. But choose your best friends, and be faithful to them. Don't worry about pleasing everyone else. A friend loves at all times, but you can't love your friends fully if you're too busy trying to walk with everyone.

Jesus wasn't best friends with everyone. He sat and ate with all types of people and wasn't exclusive, but He had a close circle that He spent each day with. There's not room for everyone to be in your close circle.

So do yourself a favor: take a deep breath. Now tell yourself, *You can't be everyone's best friend.* This truth gives you the freedom to make real, deep friendships. For everyone else, focus on being kind more than on being liked. When you live to be liked, you end up with many shallow acquaintances and no friends who know the real you.

Dear Father, help me choose my best friends wisely and commit myself to deep relationships with them. Give me the boldness to walk away from anyone You do not want in my future. Help me focus on loving and not trying to be liked. Amen.

6 THINGS TO LOOK FOR IN A FRIEND

1. SOMEONE WHO MAKES YOUR BAD DAYS BETTER.

2. SOMEONE WHO IS GENTLE WITH YOUR FEELINGS BUT BOLD WITH THEIR ACCOUNTABILITY.

3. SOMEONE WHO CELEBRATES YOUR WINS.

4. SOMEONE WHO PUSHES YOU TO BE KINDER AND INCLUSIVE.

5. SOMEONE WHO DOESN'T ACT BETTER THAN YOU BUT DOES INSPIRE YOU TO BE BETTER.

6. SOMEONE WHO HAS SEEN YOU DANCING LIKE A FOOL WITHOUT MAKEUP AND STILL HYPES YOU UP LIKE YOU DESERVE.

FOCUS ON BEING

kind
KIND

NOT ON BEING LIKED.

47

TO THE GIRL SURROUNDED
BY NEGATIVITY

Jesus entered the temple courts and drove out all who were
buying and selling there. He overturned the tables of the
money changers and the benches of those selling doves.
"It is written," he said to them, "'My house will be called a
house of prayer,' but you are making it 'a den of robbers.'"

—MATTHEW 21:12–13

When I was younger, my friend group always gossiped. They talked about everyone and never in a positive light. There were constant snickers and mean words. I tried to not join them, but I slowly became one of them. Their negatively caught on, and I also became a gossip.

Then one day as I left the lunch table, I heard one girl make a comment about me: "No wonder no guy likes Grace." I didn't hear the full sentence, but it was enough to know they were talking about me negatively. Why was I even surprised? Still, I cried.

When you're surrounded by negative people, you become a negative person. You also become a target for their negativity. And that's frustrating.

See, Jesus once walked into the temple, the Jews' place of worship, and saw people selling things needed for sacrifices at high prices. The sellers were taking advantage of worshipers for profit. They were using the temple for the wrong reason, so Jesus flipped their tables over. Jesus gets frustrated too! His anger is always righteous, and His anger is always just, but His anger is real. He doesn't like negativity.

Like the sellers in the temple, people often use the church for the wrong reasons. This happens a lot with gossip. I know for me, gossip has taken place at church, whether through prayer requests or through catching up. Jesus feels the same way today about religious people taking advantage of His children and making themselves stronger at others' expense. If you walk with Jesus and accept Him in your heart, your tables and conversations—whether at church or not—should be about caring for others and showing love.

YOU WILL BECOME LIKE THE PEOPLE YOU SURROUND YOURSELF WITH. If your people hurt others, you will slip into their ways. You will also be hurt by them. Anyone who gossips with you probably also gossips about you. Spend time with people who cheer others on, not with people who tear others down.

Who surrounds you? Stop ignoring others' negativity and meanness. Stand up for kindness, then be bold and walk away from any tables that Jesus would have flipped.

Dear God, help me to walk away from tables You would have flipped. Help me to have Your love and be a positive person. Bring me people who are like a "house of prayer." Amen.

48

TO THE GIRL HURT BY A CHRISTIAN

We love because he first loved us.

—1 JOHN 4:19

Recently, I got a mean comment on an old Instagram post. So I rushed to the profile of the lady who made fun of my looks and voice. Guess what her bio said? 1 John 4:19.

Like, excuse me? Did you miss the memo when you left that not-so-loving comment on my post? I was more frustrated by her bio saying she was a Christian than I was by the hurtful post. And it reminded me of the day one of my bullies showed up to my youth group. *Can't he go to another church?* I'd thought. *Someone, please tell this bully that he doesn't get to just accept Christ and then pretend he never hurt me.* I was mad to see him there!

I know that's not kind, but being hurt stings worse when it comes from someone who claims to follow Christ. But the truth is, we don't love people in hopes that they'll be nice, think we're awesome, and be our friends. And we don't love just the nice people. We love the hater and the bully and the frenemy who talks down to us. We don't love people because they love us, we love them because Christ loves us.

Remind yourself—Jesus was betrayed. Jesus was hurt by people who claimed to be His friends. He knows exactly how you feel. But Jesus taught to "turn to them the other cheek also" (Matthew 5:38–40). Notice He didn't say, "Expect karma to come" or "You'll show him up one day." He said to make yourself vulnerable to more hurt. A slap is an insult. It stings our hearts more than our skin. So this teaching means that we shouldn't react to personal slights. (It does *not* mean to let yourself get beat up!) Be the more Christlike person. Love that bully, even though they'll likely hurt you again.

Someone once told me, "There's nothing worse than being walked on." I disagree. I desire to live a life of love that reflects Jesus. Chances are, that means I'm gonna get walked on occasionally. I pray that after those moments I love those people anyway.

Loving a bully doesn't mean trusting them. It means being vulnerable enough to get walked on again. What's worse than getting walked on? Living a life that doesn't reflect Jesus. There will be nothing worse than standing before Jesus and having to confess, "I could have loved more." So let's be Christians who are more scared of a life that doesn't love well than a life that gets walked on. You'll never regret choosing love, but you will always regret choosing revenge.

———————

Dear Father, I am hurt, and I feel let down by someone who claims to know You. I know it's not my job to punish them, but it is my opportunity to love them because You loved me. I am undeserving of Your love, so I will love others who are undeserving of my love. Help me do this. Amen.

TO THE GIRL WITH A NON-CHRISTIAN FRIEND OR RELATIVE

When Jesus saw their faith, he said,
"Friend, your sins are forgiven."

—LUKE 5:20

I had a friend in high school who I always prayed would accept Jesus. I invited her to church, but she came only once. She was honest with me that faith wasn't her thing. Finally, instead of trying to talk to her about Jesus, I just talked to her about life. When we graduated, we went our separate ways, and I didn't see her for about eight years. Then one time I was in my hometown and another friend said she had reconnected with this girl, so we all went to the Mexican restaurant we used to go to as teenagers. While there, this old friend told me she had a dream about me and wanted to talk about faith.

I was floored. I had prayed for an opportunity to watch this friend consider the gospel, and here it was. We caught up, ate lots of queso, and talked about Jesus. Her heart was seeking Him.

There's a story in the Bible about a group of friends, one of whom couldn't walk. Some of his friends heard about Jesus healing people, so they brought the man to where Jesus was speaking. But there was a crowd, and they realized the only way to get to Jesus was to go through the roof of the house He was inside. So they made an opening in the roof and lowered their friend down in front of Jesus. Jesus healed the man of his sins first, then of his illness. Jesus said He had healed the man because of the friends' faith.

Sometimes we put so much pressure on bringing our friends to church. That's a great thing to try, but I love this story because the friends brought their faith to this man first. They told him about Jesus, then picked him up and carried him to Jesus.

Maybe you're praying for your sibling or your parents to accept Christ. Maybe you want to talk about Jesus to a friend. Have faith, bring them to Jesus as they are, pray, and wait. Your faith can change your friend's or family member's heart. But you don't have to always talk about Jesus with them. Live alongside them. Wait for an opportunity. Then show your faith boldly. And be prepared to adventure through unexpected obstacles and conversations to bring them to Jesus.

Dear Savior, thank You for what You have done in my life. I pray for opportunities to go through roofs for my friends and family members and bring them to You. I will trust Your timing and be ready. I pray for ___ right now. Soften their heart so they can be prepared to hear about You. Amen.

TO THE GIRL HOLDING A GRUDGE

Do not repay evil with evil or insult with insult. On the
contrary, repay evil with blessing, because to this you
were called so that you may inherit a blessing.

—1 PETER 3:9

I was scrolling on Instagram when I saw her. She was the not-so-nice girl from high school now grown up. She had started off as my friend, but after a series of events that included her gossiping about me, saying some hurtful things, and betraying my trust, we stopped being friends. I saw her profile and I am disgusted with what I did next. I screenshotted her picture and texted a friend: "Classic Allie, posing so forced . . . who does she think she is?" The name is obviously changed, but the comment is true. And it sounds like a textbook mean-girl insult. I insulted the way she was standing as if that was an excuse to pick on her.

That was a nasty thing to do, but I bet many of you have also screen-shotted a picture and sent it to a group text to insult, gossip, or throw some low blows. Sometimes when we get hurt, we hold a grudge instead of moving on. A simple tension you have with an old friend, an ex, a family member, or a teacher will turn ugly when you hold a grudge. Bitterness is ugly.

A couple of years back, I was furloughed during a mass phone call. I had worked for that company for over two years, and I was upset that they let me go in a way that made me feel more like an email address than a person. At first I held a grudge. I was hurt. But then I realized that as long as I held a grudge, I couldn't move on. Stuck in bitterness, I couldn't find peace or even see my present blessings.

You've been hurt, yes. But you've also been loved. Instead of holding a grudge, hold on to the truth that you are loved by a God who is good at being God. You don't need to get revenge and stalk that mean girl's profile waiting to see her fail. Pray for your enemies. Pray for those who hurt you (Matthew 5:44). Instead of holding a grudge, give out grace and love and live with a free heart.

Dear Jesus, I feel bitterness in my heart right now. Will You forgive me for holding a grudge and give me the goodness to offer grace and love instead? Help me remember Your love for me so I can love others. I pray that those who have hurt me will feel peace and love from my presence. Amen.

TO THE GIRL WANTING TO BE LOYAL

"Where you go I will go, and where you stay I will stay.
Your people will be my people and your God my God.
Where you die I will die, and there I will be buried."

—RUTH 1:16–17

When I was seventeen, I got invited to a party with the exclusive girls from my school. The weekend of the party, a friend asked me to hang out. Sarah had been loyal to me for so long, but I lied to her and said I was busy with my family. Then I went to the party that I knew Sarah wasn't invited to. Sarah saw where I was on Snapchat and realized I had lied to her. I felt awful that I hadn't been loyal to her.

Sometimes you get invited to the cool party, and other times you don't. Seasons change. But your character and legacy stay forever. When you choose dishonesty over loyalty, you'll feel disgusted with yourself. After I hurt Sarah, I tried to be a better friend.

The story of Ruth in the Bible is a perfect example of loyalty. Through a long series of events, Ruth lost her husband and all the male relatives in her household. In her culture, that meant she'd lost everyone who would have provided for her needs. Her mother-in-law advised Ruth to leave and find a new husband to take care of her. After all, that's what the culture said to do in that circumstance. But Ruth said this: "Where you go, I will go."

Ruth cared more about her mother-in-law than she cared about doing what was normal—even though that meant she would be poor. Ruth stuck to Naomi instead of looking after herself and leaving the older woman alone. She chose love.

God calls us to be loving. You aren't called to follow your friends or follow the culture. GOD DOESN'T CARE WHAT'S "NORMAL." And I truly believe that when you live out loyalty and love, you'll find blessings. It may not be an invite to the party or a popular prom date—it will be something better because it will come from your loving Father. Ruth's loyalty and love led her to the blessing of a good man who changed her life. Let me be clear: I'm not promising that you will get a popular boyfriend tomorrow and have a TikTok go viral all because you were loyal. In fact, I think God's blessings are better than our worldly desires. But God does care to bless His faithful children. So be expectant. When you live a loving and loyal life, you'll realize that your God is loyal to you.

Be a good friend. Be loyal. Listen to God, and expect big blessings to come.

Dear God, help me live a loyal and loving life like Ruth. Help me choose loyalty over popularity or being "normal." Lead me to Your blessings that come from choosing kindness over cool. Amen.

TO THE GIRL FRUSTRATED WITH SOMEONE

A hot-tempered person stirs up conflict, but
the one who is patient calms a quarrel.

—PROVERBS 15:18

There was a time when I didn't get along with my mom. Anything she said would set me off. I was always frustrated with her. *Why did she ask about my college applications again? Why does she still need to know when I get home? Why doesn't she remember that I hate pork chops?*

My frustration with my mom grew, and soon others were pushing my buttons too: teachers, coworkers, friends. I was impatient with everyone. And when I stopped giving grace to others, I also stopped giving grace to myself. I thought my frustration validated my negative emotions, but really, my frustration caused me to lose control over my emotions. I often spewed out words I didn't mean, and I was always in a state of internal chaos.

As I got older, I realized that my mom wasn't perfect, but she was try-ing. She was loving, and she cared. She didn't always say the right thing, but life isn't about being right; it's about being love. I know it is impossible to always get along with parents or siblings, and frustration is a normal feeling. **BUT GIVING GRACE WILL ALWAYS BRING PEACE.** When you give grace to others instead of giving them a piece of your frustrated mind, you will bring peace to the relationship and to your own mind.

My frustration was never going to help my relationship with my mom. She and I are alike in many ways and different in many ways, but she was never trying to get under my skin. So give grace instead of going off. If you need to walk away from a conversation to find grace, walk away. Spend time praying instead of jumping to conclusions and yelling. Once you give grace and spend more time praying before you speak, you will see that fights are really just your pride reacting to a disagreement. You aren't called to agree with everyone, but you are called to give grace to everyone.

Dear God, some relationships in my life are hard. Help me choose to give grace over giving a piece of my mind. You don't call me to agree with everyone, but I do need to be patient with everyone. My first thoughts aren't always true thoughts or kind thoughts, so help me react with self-control and speak Your Spirit instead of speaking my mind when someone frustrates me. Amen.

53

TO THE GIRL WITH A FRIEND
MAKING BAD CHOICES

Brothers and sisters, if someone is caught in a sin, you
who live by the Spirit should restore that person gently.
But watch yourselves, or you also may be tempted.

—GALATIANS 6:1

I had a friend I had known since I was little. At a sleepover in middle school, we told each other that we would follow God in high school. However, as we got older, she made bad choices. Slowly, she walked away from Christ. She became boy crazy, did drugs, and partied. She gossiped and hurt others, including me. At first I tried to call her out. I told her what she was doing was wrong. When that didn't work, I distanced myself from her. Finally, I tried to be friends with her again, but her company caused me to fall.

You may have someone in your life who is going down a bad path. It's easy to think you should call them out, and it's even easier to join them. But call your friends up, not out. Calling out treats others with disgust and focuses on the bad. Calling up treats others with love and gentleness. LOVE CHANGES PEOPLE'S HEARTS. When you call someone up, you show them what matters and who is over it all: the Author of love—Jesus. Don't give up on your friend, but stop hanging out with her so much if you need to. It's a lot easier to be pulled down than to bring someone up.

Also, find friends who are trying to walk the path of faith. It will be a lot easier to resist the peer pressure of one friend when you have a group that is seeking God's higher purpose.

Follow Jesus' example. He spent His days with a core group of friends who were seeking God, but He also spent time with shady people known to be thieves and prostitutes. Jesus sat with them, listened to them, and called them to leave their sin behind.

You, too, can be a light to someone making bad choices. Show them Jesus by listening to them, being there for them, and lovingly telling them the truth about their actions (Ephesians 4:15). Don't worry about speaking the perfect words, and don't feel like you have to give your friend the same amount of your presence as before. Let the light of Jesus shine through your good actions and big love. Call up, not out, and make sure you are surrounded with people who show you the light named Jesus.

If your friends are going down a dark path, pray for them, love them, and press on toward Jesus. Be the light, don't chase the darkness.

Dear Jesus, help me call my friend up and not out. I pray I can show my friend Your beautiful grace. Help them see and hear Your light in me, even through the darkness. And help me find people who are also shining Your light. Amen.

54

TO THE GIRL WITHOUT A BEST FRIEND

But if we walk in the light, as he is in the light,
we have fellowship with one another.

—1 JOHN 1:7

I once lived with two girls who were inseparable. Don't get me wrong, they were nice and would invite me to hang with them at times. But let's be real, I was the third wheel. They were each other's best friend, and I was over there on the outside. I was in my twenties but still felt like the girl watching everyone else pick a project partner. It's not fun to stand on the side watching everyone find their "person."

Shows always have awesome friend groups, and everyone seems to have a best friend. But that's not always how life is. I have my go-to friends and friends I consider to be my best friends, but I don't have one BFF. There's no one attached to my hip, and maybe that's not a bad thing.

God is going to lead you to amazing people, and I hope you find friendships that make you feel known and give you comfort when you go through heartbreak, grief, and a hard year. But I hope that you don't put your happiness in one person. Life isn't about finding a friend group or finding a best friend and only hanging out with them. Life is about finding good people, being loving, and walking with the confidence that you aren't alone.

I pray you find best friends, but I also pray you aren't so attached to one person or group that you miss out on loving and being loved by others. Maybe you don't have a singular "best friend" because God has given you some important friendships from all over that He wants you to appreciate. Maybe God doesn't want you to be overcommitted to one person and miss out on the couple of amazing friends who call you up. It's okay if you don't have a go-to partner for life. In God's timing you will find peace in your friendships. But until then, walk boldly, love big, and remind yourself you aren't missing out because your life doesn't look like your Netflix watchlist.

Dear God, some people seem to always have a go-to best friend, and I sometimes feel left out. Help me pour into the people in my life now and not try to be someone's favorite. Remind me to walk boldly, love big, and be a good friend to those You have given me, even if I'm not someone's best friend right now. Amen.

5 REMINDERS FOR THE GIRL
READY TO SHARE HER LOVE

1. IT'S OKAY TO NOT TRUST EVERYONE. GIVE EVERYONE GRACE AND LOVE, BUT GIVE TRUST ONLY WITH WISDOM AND DISCERNMENT.

2. DON'T LET YOUR PAST HURTS STOP YOU FROM LOVING PEOPLE IN YOUR PRESENT.

3. FRIENDSHIP DOESN'T HAPPEN OVERNIGHT. IT STARTS WITH A HELLO AND IS ABOUT SHOWING UP IN ALL SEASONS.

4. STOP TRYING TO SQUEEZE INTO TABLES. CREATE YOUR OWN TABLE, AND BE THE INCLUSIVE FRIEND.

5. THERE ARE NO CLIQUES IN HEAVEN. HAVE SOME GO-TO FRIENDS, BUT DON'T OUTCAST ANYONE.

55

TO THE GIRL STRESSING OUT

"Come to me, all you who are weary and
burdened, and I will give you rest."

—MATTHEW 11:28

One night I was in the library at 2 a.m. cramming for finals. I was chugging Diet Coke, trying to teach myself irregular verbs in Swahili, and overthinking about the guy I was talking to. Then I began to cry—not just because of the boy or because of my tests. I was crying because of it *all*.

Maybe school is kicking your butt or your friendships are on the rocks. Maybe your planner is full, and you feel like you can never stop. Maybe the rumors are exhausting, and you want one day without dumb drama. You might tell yourself these things aren't a big deal, but when you try to carry them all, they get heavier and heavier.

It's like a water bottle. If I held a water bottle up in the air, it would seem light. Maybe I could hold it up for ten minutes. But if I tried to hold it up for two hours—yeah, that little bottle would feel *heavy*.

Jesus called the weary to bring their burdens to Him, and He promised rest. Notice He didn't say, "Come to me all you who finished the year with a GPA higher than gas prices." He didn't say, "Come to me after you go hard, join all the clubs, and prove yourself." He invited all who are "weary and burdened."

You were not meant to carry your burdens. You *can't* carry your burdens. But Jesus can. Instead of feeling stressed, give your stress to your Savior. Give Him your nerves, your fears, and your frustrations. Trade your load for the peace that comes from trusting your Savior with your concerns.

Find true rest in Jesus. Rest isn't a prize you earn come Christmas break or graduation or after you win that election. And rest isn't sleeping in or practicing yoga. It's releasing your burdens to Jesus and living in His peace. You don't have to earn rest; CHRIST HOLDS REST OUT TO YOU.

So on the Tuesdays you feel overwhelmed, look down. See those two feet God gave you? They've walked many halls, through many overwhelming days and through a lot of pain. God has walked with you this far; trust Him to continue by your side. Give God your burdens, and walk with the rest that comes from knowing the peace of God's presence.

Dear God, I know I wasn't meant to hold on to anything from the world. I give You my burdens. Help me see You, even when life is busy, and walk in Your rest. Amen.

56

TO THE GIRL WITH BIG EMOTIONS

When Jesus saw her weeping, and the Jews who had come
along with her also weeping, he was deeply moved in spirit
and troubled. "Where have you laid him?" he asked.
"Come and see, Lord," they replied.
Jesus wept.
Then the Jews said, "See how he loved him!"

—JOHN 11:33–36

Fun fact about me: I cry. I cry when watching sappy wedding videos, and I cry when I talk to my grandma because she is adorable. I cried at the ending of *Shrek*. I don't know why. And when my friend was going through a breakup, I cried watching her doubt her worth.

I used to be embarrassed that I was a crier. I thought being emotional was a bad thing.

Many girls think they need to hide their feelings and apologize for their emotions. And for this, I am sorry. You are a human being. Sometimes you will be sad, hurt, angry, and lonely. Sometimes you will be happy, grateful, or touched by something beautiful. Emotions are normal. God often uses our emotions to speak to us.

The shortest verse in the Bible is "Jesus wept." This short verse is also one of the most powerful. Jesus had heard that His friend Lazarus was dead, and He went to visit Lazarus's family. Lazarus's body was already in a tomb. Jesus knew He was about to raise Lazarus from the dead, but He still cried when He saw his dead friend. Jesus didn't hide His emotions and try to be chill. Everyone in the town noticed that His emotions were real, and they understood that Jesus' tears showed His love.

Jesus cried, and so can you. Jesus was frustrated, and you can feel frustrated. Jesus showed His hurt, His righteous anger, His compassion, and His sadness countless times. Emotions are often a sign of a big heart. So if you wear your heart on your sleeve, that's okay. You feel the hurt others face because of your genuine love. When you have the joy of the Lord, you also have His compassion.

Dear Jesus, thank You for modeling how beautiful emotions can be. Remind me that letting myself express sadness, frustration, hurt, and compassion is a good thing. I pray I can find You in my emotions. I pray that my emotions represent my love and not my selfishness. Amen.

57

TO THE GIRL UNDER PRESSURE

I press on to take hold of that for which Christ Jesus took hold of me.... Forgetting what is behind and straining toward what is ahead, I press on toward the goal to win the prize for which God has called me heavenward in Christ Jesus.

—PHILIPPIANS 3:12–14

Parents and bosses, coaches and teachers, friends and boys. So many people have expectations of us. And sometimes they are just too much.

One time in high school, my mom told me to take Spanish 3. She pushed me with good intentions. She just wanted me to be successful. But I was horrible at Spanish, and I knew that class wasn't something I wanted to do. Yet instead of being honest about how hard this subject was for me, I took the class—and struggled all year long.

Another time, I was dating a guy who pressured me to have sex. I remember thinking that I was a bad girlfriend because I wouldn't give him what he wanted. I didn't give in completely, but I went further with him than I wanted. I listened to his voice more than what my heart knew to be right.

You may feel pressure from your parents too. Or maybe you've been in that situation with a guy. Maybe your friends pressure you to drink or do drugs, or your coach pushes you to win by any means necessary. Pressure isn't a fun feeling. And this discomfort often leads us to mold ourselves into the people others want us to be instead of who God wants us to be.

I don't think anyone is trying to be mean when they pressure us. Usually their pressure comes from their own insecurity or sin. They want us to be our best without asking what's really best for us. Or they're seeking to fulfill a need that they should be satisfying in God. But even when pressure comes from love, you don't have to give in. Be bold enough to stand firm in who Christ made you to be. Have the courage to press forward toward Him instead of caving to pressure from others.

Don't be afraid to be honest with those who pressure you. Tell your parents if their expectations don't match who you know yourself to be. Don't be afraid to walk away from a relationship that is dependent on physical intimacy. Be real with your friends—true friends will respect your choices. Pressure pushes you down, but pressing forward to Christ brings you closer to His holiness, kindness, and peace.

Dear Lord Jesus, help me identify when I am feeling pressure to do things that aren't best for me. Give me the boldness to tell others when their words or actions make me uncomfortable. I want to press forward toward You instead of trying to be who others want me to be. Amen.

58

TO THE GIRL PRETENDING SHE'S FINE

The LORD is a refuge for the oppressed,
a stronghold in times of trouble.
—PSALM 9:9

I got a call from a friend, and my heart dropped at what she told me. She had gone to a party, and a guy gave her a strong drink. She blacked out and woke up in his bed naked. She was raped. When she called me crying, I drove to her, took her to the hospital, and listened to her tears.

Afterward she avoided talking about her pain and hurt. My heart broke for her. Although I had never been raped, I knew what it was like to be hurt by someone and pretend to be fine. I watched my friend try to numb the pain through alcohol, partying, and guys. She blamed herself for what happened, but it was *not* her fault. She did not give consent. Someone else's sin is never your fault.

The Bible does not say "thou shalt always be fine." It is not a sin to be sad and hurt. God doesn't want anyone to be in pain, but this world is broken, and people's sins hurt others.

Still, it's possible to experience peace even in the "not fine." After that awful night, my friend struggled to find peace, but she looked in the wrong places. Peace comes from finding the One who has it all together, even when your life is falling apart. When you feel oppressed and get hurt by someone's sin, God doesn't need a "fine" you. He wants an honest you. YOU CAN'T BE HEALED IF YOU DON'T FIRST ADMIT YOU HAVE BEEN HURT. But when you take your pain to God, He will surround you like the stone walls of the fortress—or "stronghold"—that the psalmist wrote about.

And if your friend has been hurt, she doesn't need you to promise "it gets better" a million times. She needs someone who hears her and points her to God, who is a stronghold of safety. You don't have to be strong to find peace during times of trouble. All you need is your mighty God who can protect you from more pain.

So when you get hurt, tell someone. Cry and express your feelings. And trust that God is strong even when you are not. Peace isn't exclusive to the times your life feels easy and restful. Peace is found through knowing your strong God.

Dear God, thank You for being strong even when I'm not. Remind me that someone else's sin against me isn't my fault. Help me be honest about the hurt I feel and allow You to be my safe stronghold. My pain is real, but peace comes from having You in my life, not from having an easy life. Amen.

TO THE GIRL READY FOR REST

It was very early in the morning and still dark.
Jesus got up and left the house. He went to a place
where he could be alone. There he prayed.

—MARK 1:35 NIrV

It's hard for me to rest. I remember hating nap time in kindergarten, but now I wish nap time was still a thing. My life often feels like it never stops, and it's been that way for a long time. In high school, I juggled clubs, sports, and a job. On the nights I worked as a waitress, I had only one hour between when I got home from school and when I had to get to work.

I went through a phase when I used this hour to watch a show called *Criminal Minds*. I was a sixteen-year-old who loved pink, dancing, and being silly, and I was watching a show about creepy murders during my only break. As if crazy criminals were restful! I don't know why I did it, but the show was addictive.

While my body was physically resting, my mind was filling with horror and fear.

I think we have forgotten that true rest isn't a nap, TV time, or sitting on the couch. Rest that calms the soul comes from going to a silent place and allowing God to be louder than the world for a minute. I know what you're thinking: *but God doesn't actually speak.* He may not be a voice you can hear, but when you find time alone in silence to pray, you will begin to feel His presence. When you open His Word without rushing, you will notice things you haven't seen before.

Jesus modeled rest for us. Between two of His miracles, He and his disciples went to a quiet place and prayed. Several times, the Bible mentions that Jesus went off to pray. He did this regularly, no matter what else was going crazy in His day. So whether life slows down or not, you need rest. There's nothing wrong with watching television shows or listening to music or texting friends. But when your life is hectic, remember that the rest you really need comes from God. Like Jesus, you need to go to a quiet place and pray. Rest isn't earned, and it isn't a prize you should only receive come summer or when you get a break from school or your job. Rest is holy and something Jesus modeled. So turn off the TV and take a moment to rest your soul.

Dear Father, I need to take time regularly to turn off my mind. Help me find time and a quiet place to talk to You honestly. My life is hectic, but I always need Your rest. Amen.

60

TO THE GIRL TRYING TO HANDLE IT ALL

Jesus looked at them and said to them, "With men this
is impossible, but with God all things are possible."
—MATTHEW 19:26 NKJV

I can't do this. I looked at my red, wet face in the bathroom mirror. I was struggling with anxious thoughts about finals. I felt like I would never be able to feel peace in the middle of my test week. School used to come easy for me. Until it didn't.

Another time I was in a high-stress job with a tough workload. Each day, my anxious thoughts increased. I tried to handle it on my own. I wanted to handle it. But then one day at lunch with my parents, I broke down and cried.

I used to love the quote "God doesn't give you more than you can handle." I would journal it, doodle it, and I'm pretty sure I had it on a sticky note in my bathroom. But there were things in my life that I, Grace, could *not* handle. I could not handle my anxious thoughts during certain classes. I could not handle the pressure of that job. I needed help to bear those things. I needed a Savior to carry my heavy load, and I needed people to point me to the Prince of Peace. (FYI, that saying about what we can handle is *not* in the Bible. It's a distortion of 1 Corinthians 10:13.)

I can promise you that in this life you will have hard days. You will have trials (John 16:33). Death will steal some of the greatest people you know. School will overwhelm you, and your job will stress you out. Illness sometimes ruins our plans, and every now and then heartbreak sneaks into our souls and takes our joy. And you cannot heal properly by smiling and hoping life gets better. You can't always just power through. I am not promising that God won't give you more than you can handle. What I am promising is that GOD WON'T GIVE YOU MORE THAN *HE* CAN HANDLE. He is with you through your storm. He is there for you, and He so desperately wants you to cling to Him when life gets hard.

It is impossible to find peace on your own, but with God, anything is possible. Today may be a hard chapter, but your God is good, and your God is big. Stop trying to handle it all on your own. You *cannot* handle it on your own. You need to be honest about your struggle. Be honest with yourself, and ask for Christ's power to help you press on. Be honest with a few close relatives or friends so they can help you and point you to Christ. You can't, but God can.

Dear God, I know You can do anything, and what is impossible for me is possible for You. Help me through the hard and show me people in my life I can trust and who will point me to You. Lord, I am so thankful I don't have to handle it all on my own. Amen.

61

TO THE GIRL OVERTHINKING

"Be strong and courageous. Do not fear or be in dread of them, for it is the LORD your God who goes with you. He will not leave you or forsake you."

—DEUTERONOMY 31:6 ESV

I have a friend who went skydiving recently. Anna showed me the video, and as I watched her jump out of the plane, she seemed kind of scared, but she also effortlessly jumped. I wondered if I could do that. Then I started to think of all the things that could happen: the parachute could get stuck and not open; I could land in a tree; a bird could attack me. . . . Oops, I was doing it again—overthinking. I am not a jumper; I am an overthinker.

I am constantly overthinking every situation. My inner monologue sounds like this: *Do I reply to this text with an exclamation point, or is that trying too hard? Will I be the only one wearing a dress to dinner? If I post three stories on Instagram, will everyone be annoyed? If I go on this trip, will I miss out on something better? If I go to this event, will I have anyone to talk to, or will I be in the corner playing on my phone feeling awkward?* Yeah, it's a lot.

So I asked Anna how she had the nerve to jump out of the plane like that. Wasn't she scared?

"Yeah, I was scared," Anna said, "but I knew I wasn't alone."

Anna explained that there was an experienced skydiver on her back who was in charge of her jump. So yes, she was jumping, but she jumped with someone who knew what they were doing. This person was experienced, not afraid, and was with her the whole time.

Are you an overthinker like me? Are you currently imagining another worst-case scenario? Or maybe you're overthinking about next year when you have to switch schools or get a job. Maybe you're overthinking and worried about a game, a college choice, or a big test. Whatever is causing you to overthink, instead of freaking out about the jump, remember you are not alone. The God who created you is guiding you. The jump is scary, but God is with you. With Him, the jump, the new, and the hard can go from being scary to being an adventurous journey full of new and exciting things.

Dear God, I trust that You're with me, even when I can't see You. I pray that, instead of overthinking, I will remember that I am jumping through the crazy with You, the God over it all. Remind me that I do not need to be afraid, because You are with me. Teach me to find adventure in the unknown instead of staying in fear. Amen.

4 THOUGHTS ON OVERTHINKING

1. RATHER THAN SEEKING TO UNDERSTAND WHAT'S NEXT, SEEK TO SEE JESUS IN YOUR NEXT.

2. GOD IS GOOD AT BEING GOD.

3. YOU ARE NOT ALONE. BRING YOUR FEAR TO JESUS.

4. THERE IS ADVENTURE IN THE UNKNOWN. GOD WILL USE CHANGE AND DISCOMFORT FOR YOUR GOOD.

TRYING TO HANDLE IT

STOP

ALL ON YOUR OWN.

62

TO THE GIRL READY TO LET GO

Temptation comes from our own desires, which entice us
and drag us away. These desires give birth to sinful actions.
And when sin is allowed to grow, it gives birth to death.

—JAMES 1:14–15 NLT

Fun fact about me: I mow my lawn. At first this was a cute little fact about me. I bought my tiny house in Orlando, painted the door pink, and trimmed the grass. I like being independent, but after a while, I think I started praying for a husband more than usual—one who enjoyed yard work.

One summer I put off mowing my lawn for three months. First my lawn mower broke. . . . Then I got busy. . . . Then the next thing I knew, my grass was very high. Finally, my sweet neighbor brought over a weed whacker. I told her she didn't have to help; I was the one to blame. But she said, "No, we all need help sometimes." When she helped, the chore went a lot faster.

So now there's you. Maybe it started as one hit on a vape, one gossip sesh, one lie, or one night at his house. What starts as one yes to something toxic can grow out of control if you don't do two things: tend to your spirit and receive help.

In college I got stuck in a cycle of gossiping and drinking too much. I stopped going to church and slowly stopped praying. Then one day I realized I was far away from Christ. It felt like there were weeds in my life. I tried to get back to God on my own, but it was hard. I would go along for a time and then look at my life and think, *Now it's worse*. Finally, I asked for help from a Christian mentor and Christian friends. When I had help from others, it was easier to clean up my mess and tend my spirit. With their encouragement, I started saying no to gossip and partying. And I spent more time with God in prayer and reading His Word. Day by day, I cut back the weeds and fed the beautiful things growing in my life.

Prayer and community throughout your day go a long way. What might seem like a simple prayer or a quick check-in with a Christian friend is tending your faith, like when I lightly mow my grass. It's easier to avoid the toxic weeds of sin when you tend to your relationship with Christ. But if it has been a while and you feel choked by sin, remember that there are people who want to help you tend your heart. Don't try to do it by yourself. Ask for help.

Dear God, sometimes I don't tend to the weeds of sin in my life. I want to do a better job of staying in communication with You and Christian community instead of letting sin choke out my faith. Help me find the people around me who can help me. Amen.

63

TO THE GIRL ATTACHED TO HER PHONE

*Who is wise? Let them realize these things. Who is discerning?
Let them understand. The ways of the LORD are right; the
righteous walk in them, but the rebellious stumble in them.*

—HOSEA 14:9

After college, I was a girls' minister for high schoolers at a church. One of my favorite times was Wednesday nights when I led a small group of guys and girls. We shared laughs, and it was a wide range of people.

I was at this group one day when a text with my college friends was lighting up. We were all sharing Snapchat memories from formal and texting about old memories, now not-that-cute dresses, and stupid boys. I was laughing at my phone when one of my students said: "Grace, your phone never turns off. I bet you're attached."

I explained that this was a one-time thing. I was *not* addicted to my phone.

Here's the thing: I wouldn't have blinked if my mom called me out for being on my phone or if my grandma joked, "Grace is *alwayyyyys* on her phone." But a fifteen-year-old had said this. So I was humbled yet still in denial. Then my students told me that you can view how many hours a day you spend on Instagram. I begged them not to make me look. But we did. Let's just say that when I saw the number, there was no denying that I *was* attached to my phone.

Phones can be a good thing. They connect us to friends who live far away and keep our parental figures from worrying about us when we're out. BUT A GOOD THING CAN TURN INTO A BAD THING IF IT IS NOT A GOD THING.

I've learned that I'm more stressed if I'm always emailing or texting. I'm more insecure after scrolling on social media for a long time. I've learned, through discernment and prayer, the importance of having one day a week when I use my phone only for emergencies. On this day, I shut off my apps. When I find myself itching for my phone, I write down a prayer.

Have you prayed about how you use your phone and how it affects you? Prayer changes our perspective. When we pray about the things we struggle with, God will bring us wisdom, self-control, goodness, and faithfulness. And go ahead and check that count of how much time you spend on your apps or phone. You might be surprised.

The next time your scrolling finger itches, first take the time to write an honest prayer and seek God's wisdom about your behavior.

Dear Lord, give me the discernment to know when my phone is an obsession and not just a tool. Help me be honest with myself about why I think I need my phone. Help me add a time to my day and my week when I turn off my notifications and find peace in who You are. Amen.

64

TO THE GIRL REFUSING TO BE STILL

He says, "Be still, and know that I am God; I will be exalted
among the nations, I will be exalted in the earth."

—PSALM 46:10

Once my dad was driving me to the airport. At the time, I felt overwhelmed because I was overcommitting. He could tell I was spread thin. He looked at me and said, "People like you and me have to be careful. It's important for us to be still often because we can burn ourselves out."

I needed my dad to tell me the world would keep spinning without me hustling trying to do it all. See, God is good at being God. You are called to be a light, but He doesn't need your help doing *all* the things. He's got the world, but He also wants you. So find time each day to slow down and connect with the God who is in control.

When you never stop moving, you often lead your heart astray. Your focus is on your to-do list: grades, sports, work, your follower count, and more, and you start walking away from God. Often we don't choose to walk away from God, we just get distracted. We're so busy with our everyday hustle that we forget what—and who—really matters.

Being still is not a big-kid version of time-out. No one is asking you to turn off the lights, sit in the corner, and freeze. Being still means stepping away from your to-do list, finding a quiet place to take a breather, and reflecting on who is really in control. Being still means taking a break from the chaos your days can bring, slowing down your thoughts, and giving God your full attention.

IF YOU WANT YOUR LIFE TO MAKE A DIFFERENCE, THEN YOU *MUST* BE STILL. When you take time to slow down, you give your heart and head a chance to listen to Christ over the chaos from the world. When you create quiet moments and let God into your schedule, He will give you the perspective and wisdom you need to live a purposeful life.

And be sure to not treat stillness like another task to check off. Right now (yes, now; that next thing can wait a few more minutes!) take a deep breath. Read today's verse again. What does it say about God? What does it mean for your day and your life? Scribble notes in the margins or in a journal if that helps you slow down and focus.

Okay, now what do you need to tell God or ask Him? Pray with me.

Dear God, instead of trying to do all things, I need to let go and let You be in control of all things. Help me make time to slow down and focus on You. I want to do big things for You; help me to see the tasks You have given me and to trust You'll help me with those and take care of everything else without me. Amen.

65

TO THE GIRL FACING RUMORS

Do not let any unwholesome talk come out of your mouths,
but only what is helpful for building others up according
to their needs, that it may benefit those who listen.

—EPHESIANS 4:29

One time the whole school heard that I did something bad with a guy in the bathroom at a party. The truth was, we didn't do anything. He was just watching me fix my makeup. But rumors can't be stopped. Another time a blonde college friend hooked up with a senior. Somehow the rumor spread that I had hooked up with the guy.

I've been the main topic of gossip many times, and it isn't fun. Some rumors were completely false. Some were half-truths that no one ever asked me to explain. Rumors are frustrating, and you feel like you lack any control of your own story. Gossip only leads to lies and hurt.

But I'm not blameless either. I have been way too invested in Sarah's run-in with the cops, Ethan's breakup, and the rumor about girls from my high school.

So if you are watching a rumor run out of control, take a deep breath. Gossip is a sin. Sadly, boredom leads to sins like gossip. When people have nothing better to do, they stir the pot. Other times people gossip because they're insecure and want to feel better about themselves. Give grace to everyone, even those talking about you. Maybe you can find an opportunity to share God's love with them. Also, let your hurt today make you kinder. Examine your life, and be honest about the times you, too, have gossiped and hurt others. Ask God and others for forgiveness if you need to. Last, remember that the cool girl with all the tea and the PTA moms who have nothing better to do than create prom drama are not in control of your story. Jesus is.

Also, you don't have to prove the rumor is false. Truth always wins over time. So instead of going on a social media war or trying to prove yourself, trust that God is in control of your story. Walk in truth and honor, give crazy grace, and trust Jesus' hand in your life. You are not the rumors or the gossip; you are loved. Jesus hasn't left your side.

Dear Jesus, I can't control the sins of others. The gossip and rumors hurt, but I know that You're in control. When others use words to tear me down, remind me I have a Savior who lifts me up. And the next time I start to gossip, remind me of the hurt I feel today and help me be kinder. Let my words be wholesome and holy, not destructive and mean. Amen.

66

TO THE GIRL WHOSE HOME DOESN'T FEEL LIKE HOME

The islanders showed us unusual kindness. They built a fire and welcomed us all because it was raining and cold.

—ACTS 28:2

Living with people is hard. One year in college, my roommate and I were just different. We fought over small things and big things. It's hard to share a room, share one sink, and share drama. Our dynamic reminded me of fights with my brother growing up. We would say mean words and use each other's deepest insecurities as weapons.

I've also had friends who had two homes because their parents were divorced. Each parent talked bad about the other, and my friends felt uncomfortable at each house.

It's hard to have peace when your living situation is rough. When home isn't comfortable, your whole world can feel stressful, overwhelming, and chaotic. When you have a long day and go to your room, you just want to relax. You shouldn't have to worry about anger, drama, hurtful comments, or pain. I'm so sorry if your home isn't a place of peace. You don't deserve that.

And while you may not be able to solve the problem, you might be able to make it a little better. You can be the kind one, even when things feel tense. Luke wrote in Acts about how one group of people he met left a fire going so Luke and his companion would have light and warmth. He called this kindness "unusual." God can use unusual kindness to soften hearts, heal relationships, and make a difference. Luke recorded this act over two thousand years ago, but we still read about it today.

If your living situation isn't easy, remember that Jesus is with you in the chaos. Peace isn't a quiet room or a home-cooked meal served with a hug. Peace comes when your perspective is holy. When you fix your eyes on your Savior and look past the drama, the hurt, and the latest fight, you can find peace. Because even when we can't control what life throws at us, we find peace in the knowledge that God is more powerful than any hard day.

Allow God to be the anchor for your soul so you can stand firm in any stormy situation. And maybe when others see how you have managed to find peace, they will be inspired to ask Christ to anchor them too.

Dear Jesus, when my living situation is hard, I will anchor myself in You. Help me be a light, even at home. When my home is emotionally draining, help me rest my soul in who You are. Help me control my perspective and find peace. Thank You for being in this storm with me. Amen.

7 REMINDERS FOR THE GIRL READY TO EXPERIENCE PEACE

1. PEACE IS NOT A PLACE OR FEELING. PEACE IS A PERSON NAMED JESUS.

2. REST IS BEING STILL AND KNOWING THAT GOD IS GOOD.

3. THANKFULNESS BRINGS PEACE. SOMEONE IS CURRENTLY PRAYING FOR SOMETHING YOU ALREADY HAVE. YOU MAY NOT HAVE ALL YOUR DESIRES, BUT THERE ARE BLESSINGS IN YOUR LIFE YOU HAVEN'T THANKED GOD FOR.

4. YOUR MENTAL AND SPIRITUAL HEALTH DO NOT DEPEND ON OTHERS.

5. THE PRINCE OF PEACE IS WALKING WITH YOU THROUGH THE MESSY, THE HARD, THE GOOD, AND THE CONFUSING.

6. GOD IS LEADING YOU WHERE HE MEANS YOU TO BE.

7. TRUST THAT GOD IS GOOD AT BEING GOD.

67

TO THE GIRL LACKING JOY

Sing the praises of the LORD, you his faithful people;
praise his holy name. For his anger lasts only a moment,
but his favor lasts a lifetime; weeping may stay for
the night, but rejoicing comes in the morning.

—PSALM 30:4-5

I don't like my life at all . . .

This is how I felt after my sophomore year of college. I had made some mistakes. I felt left out. School was kicking my butt. My family never seemed to get along. And I had acne, bloating, and a lot of stress . . . I did not have joy.

The past couple of years had felt this way. High school had been hard. I struggled with fitting in and felt like everyone else knew their place except me. School overwhelmed me, and I never felt like I was enough. I thought all that would go away once I got to college. I stalked colleges' websites and Instagram feeds, dreaming of the day my problems would be cured.

When I finally got to my university, I went to the football games and joined a sorority. I even made some friends who were great. But I still didn't have joy. So I went to parties hosted by cute boys. But that didn't help either. At all.

You may have days when you hate your life or life feels boring. But joy doesn't come from your circumstances. It is not something you'll experience when you graduate from high school or if you get into a sorority. You can experience joy today. I thought a change in my life would make me happy, but what I needed was a change of heart to see the joy God was offering me.

I still need to be reminded that I can claim joy each day. Recently, two popular comedians made fun of my posts on social media. At first, I broke down in an ugly, snotty cry. But then I remembered that they can't steal my joy in Christ. As I blew my nose, I prayed and told God how I felt, then I started to thank Him for all the things that matter more than what someone (even someone famous!) thinks of me: my salvation, God's presence, the opportunity to reach people across the world with His message. It didn't take long for my heart to fill with joy.

IT'S HARD TO THROW A FIT WHEN YOU'RE IN PRAYER. Prayer changes our perspective. In conversation with our heavenly Father, we can always find joy.

Dear God, I need a heart change. Help me find joy even when the world is bringing me down. My life gets filled with homework, busyness, and fear. But You are always here with me. You have it all together, even when I don't. You care when I'm down, and You want to transform any hard season into a season of joy with Your presence. Help me live in Your joy, even when life isn't going my way. Amen.

68

TO THE GIRL CRYING IN

THE BATHROOM

The LORD is near to the brokenhearted
and saves the crushed in spirit.
Many are the afflictions of the righteous, but
the LORD delivers him out of them all.
—PSALM 34:18–19 ESV

During my senior year of high school, I went to a party to hang out with the guy I was dating. But at the party I found out he had cheated on me. Oh, and I found out from his ex-girlfriend who hated me, and she told me in front of everyone. I knew I was about to cry, so I ran to the place where girls love to cry: the bathroom. I locked the door and stared in the mirror wondering, once again, why I wasn't enough.

We live in a world where girls are called "crazy" for their emotions. Our culture is obsessed with being chill. I just want to remind you that your emotions are real and so is your God. You don't have to be chill with Him—you just have to be honest. If you're not honest about the condition of your heart, how can your Savior heal your heart? Be honest about your

- 156 -- 156 -

hurt, your pain, your insecurity, and your struggle. On the days you want to run and hide your tears, know that Jesus cares. He cares about your hurt and your weariness. Run to Him.

Your tears are real, but your tears are leading to your triumph. Give them to God, and He will use them. And I'm not talking about the boy coming back or about finding great friends after you were betrayed by one. This triumph will be the day you share your heartbreak with someone and it becomes a compass that points them to God. You may be hurt today, and you may be crying in the bathroom, but one day you will watch God use your hurt to teach someone else that He cares for them.

You have a God who doesn't want you to cry alone. He cares about your hurt and wants to help you. You are loved and wanted by your God.

On that day you look in the mirror with tears in your eyes, be honest with God. Don't hide your emotions from Him. Trust that being healed is more important than pretending to be chill. You're not crazy, but you serve a crazy-big God who can help you. With Jesus, the breakups won't break you, the rejection won't name you, and you will be delivered by your God.

Dear God, my tears sometimes come fast. Thank You for being there for me. I pray to be better at not hiding my emotions from You and instead running to You. Comfort me on the days I feel sad or let down. Amen.

69

TO THE GIRL SCARED ABOUT THE FUTURE

Do not be anxious about anything, but in every situation, by
prayer and petition, with thanksgiving, present your requests to
God. And the peace of God, which transcends all understanding,
will guard your hearts and your minds in Christ Jesus.

—PHILIPPIANS 4:6-7

In middle school, I stressed about cheer tryouts. And guess what? I didn't make the team. Twice.

In high school, I was scared for a calculus test. Do you know what happened? I failed.

I was once anxious about a confrontation with a coworker. Can you guess how the conversation went? Horribly.

At each of these anxious times and many more, I stayed up late the night before trying to prepare. But I only made my stress worse, thinking through the bad that could happen instead of sleeping. And while some of the bad things I worried about happened, they often weren't as bad as I thought they would be. And even more times, something unexpectedly good happened.

Maybe you're worried about a hard test or about not being asked to the dance. Maybe you're stressing about sorority recruitment or finding new friends in your next transition. Maybe you're anxious about finding a friend to eat lunch with. Maybe you're afraid of one day getting married and having it end in divorce like your parents' marriage.

Being worried about the future is normal. However, BEING WORRIED HAS NEVER MADE THE FUTURE BETTER. Worry won't change your circumstances. And guess what? Usually, if the bad thing you imagine does happen, you'll be okay. (Really!) Because even in the bad, God leads us to good. Sometimes, the result of my situation wasn't good, but my God is always good. He can use even the hard days for your good and His glory.

Instead of being anxious, be thankful. God is working for your good! He will use all things: the loneliness, the grief, the rejection, the awkward transition, the breakup, and even the in-between pauses. I can now look back on all the twists and turns and see that there was nothing to fear. Even when doors closed and life didn't go how I wanted, my God never led me astray.

Instead of being worried about the future, pray for a better perspective about your future. That's what the apostle Paul instructed in Philippians 4. I love this passage because Paul didn't promise that things would go our way. But he did promise peace. I can't promise you that tomorrow will be easy, but when you pray, your trust and wisdom will grow. Then you will see that God is leading you to your good, and you will have peace.

Dear Father, I am worried about things I can't control. Help me slow my thoughts. And please grant me trust and wisdom. I don't know what tomorrow looks like, but I know You will be with me. I pray for Your peace and guidance. Amen.

TO THE GIRL OVERCOME WITH GRIEF

"Where, O death, is your victory?
Where, O death, is your sting?"
The sting of death is sin, and the power of sin
is the law. But thanks be to God! He gives us
the victory through our Lord Jesus Christ.

—1 CORINTHIANS 15:55-57

In high school, I was in a program that matched participants with students who had disabilities. We were called "bulldog buddies." My buddy was Jena. She loved Lady Gaga and pink just as much as I did. She was my buddy all four years, and we even went to prom together. We shopped for our girly, sparkly dresses together.

When I went to college, Jena and I talked on the phone and made sure to see each other when I was back in town. Then she got cancer. Jena had already defeated cancer twice, but it came back stronger. I prayed for God to heal her. But He didn't.

After Jena died, I was frustrated with God. I wanted to believe that He could perform miracles and that He was there in the pain. But I couldn't understand why He didn't answer my prayers for Jena.

Here's the truth: death is horrible. Death was not in God's good plan. But the world is broken by sin, and we have to deal with disease, evil, disasters, and death. Yet death isn't the end. Jesus defeated death when He came back to life! That's why death has lost its sting. Jena was a Christian, and I saw glimpses of peace when we talked about Jesus. She was experiencing so much pain, but Jesus' love on the cross gave her hope for her future. Jena knew that death is not the end for those who follow Christ. We get to share in His victory and follow Him to heaven!

This life can be heartbreaking. You may be praying for a miracle today, but there are miracles around you that you have forgotten. The greatest miracle is that Christ beat death and opened the door to heaven. In this broken world, find hope in Jesus. If we choose to follow Him, then we won't face a tombstone at the end of all this—we'll face our Savior. So take a deep breath and look up. God is more powerful than any pain you experience. This world is temporary. It's sometimes hard, sometimes fun, and always full of miracles. Each day is an opportunity to celebrate the miracles Jesus has already done and see Him make new ones.

Dear God, I don't always understand this world, and You have not always answered my prayers in the way I wanted You to. But thank You for the miracle of Jesus' resurrection that offers me salvation. Even though death is hard, I know it is not the end for those who follow You. You have the final say, not a tombstone. I trust in You, even when I feel like I have lost hope. Amen.

71

TO THE GIRL CRAVING FREEDOM

Jesus said to him, "Away from me, Satan! For it is written:
'Worship the Lord your God, and serve him only.'"
Then the devil left him, and angels
came and attended him.

—MATTHEW 4:10–11

When I was seventeen, I snuck out to my boyfriend's party three hours away. I literally lied about where I was going, convinced one friend to be reckless with me, and drove on the interstate to the party.

What started as dishonoring my parents and telling a lie led to me getting drunk, crying about how the guy slept with someone else the day before, and then still going further than I should have with him. All in one night. Isn't it crazy how one sin can domino into more? My desire to feel grown up led to my drunk self crying with hurt and regret as I realized I had made a bad choice.

When I look back on that weekend, I don't cringe, and I don't laugh. I get sad. I think of young, insecure Grace, who looked for freedom at a party. I wanted to take control of my life and get away from my parents' limits. But instead, I lost control and my parents' trust. At the time, I knew deep down that sneaking out would lead to more sins, yet I said yes anyway. The temptation was strong, and I didn't allow my relationship with Christ to be stronger.

I used to think the Bible was a list of rules. But I've realized that it's a guidebook. God doesn't ask for obedience to make us miserable. He offers His wisdom to protect us. True freedom comes from trusting that God knows what He's talking about.

Jesus once spent forty days fasting in the wilderness. During that time, the devil promised Jesus food and the idols of invincibility and power. But Jesus fought off temptation with the Word of God.

I know that you, too, are craving freedom and feeling out of control. But stop seeking control and embrace true freedom. True freedom doesn't come from sneaking out, escaping your hometown where everyone treats homecoming like it's the Met Gala, dating the guy your parents don't like, or feeling a high. True freedom comes from walking with the One who is in control, even when you aren't.

Stop trying to grow up so fast. Your innocence is beautiful. Find the freedom that comes from following God's Word and trusting that He would never keep anything good from you. His guidance isn't there to bore. It is given in love. So go find the scripture you need to fight off that temptation and believe God's promise that freedom in Christ is greater than any temporary satisfaction this world can give.

Dear Jesus, You fought off temptation with Scripture; help me do this too. I know You aren't keeping good from me: You are protecting me and giving me freedom in You. Give me a genuine heart and change my desires so I don't get stuck in temptation. Amen.

TO THE GIRL FEELING HEARTBROKEN

For I am sure that neither death nor life, nor angels nor rulers,
nor things present nor things to come, nor powers, nor height
nor depth, nor anything else in all creation, will be able to
separate us from the love of God in Christ Jesus our Lord.

—ROMANS 8:38–39 ESV

I have felt heartbroken many times. Family fights have ended with slammed doors and angry words. My romantic relationships have failed. Friends have betrayed me, and bullies have been unkind.

During homecoming season my freshman year, one guy sent a note with another guy's name asking me to the dance. I knew it was a joke, and I tried to laugh it off. But I cried for months about being a joke to my peers. When my mom asked why I didn't want to go to the dance, I didn't have the heart to tell her.

I then became obsessed with being "hot" and finding a guy to want me. Finally, a guy told me I was pretty. But that situation only led to more heartbreak.

So if you're heartbroken, I get it. Breakups suck, being left out and hurt sucks. But the cure for heartbreak isn't finding Mr. Right, making a new best friend, or cutting people out of your life. The cure for your pain is Christ.

If I could tell heartbroken Grace anything, it wouldn't be that "time heals all wounds." Heartbreak is part of this broken world, and our life stories often don't include happily ever after. Death is real, and life is hard. But I would tell heartbroken Grace that God is consistent and that He gives peace.

Maybe someone has left you or betrayed you. Maybe you feel like someone is making a joke out of you or that your love life or friendship drama is a joke. Not everyone will be consistent in your life, but you can always rely on God. God is there. HE WILL ALWAYS BE THERE. Nothing can separate you from His love. He won't wake up one day and change His mind. And there will be a day when you understand that good came out of your friend leaving, that there was a reason the relationship didn't work out, and that you became kinder because of mean bullies. The same God who carried you through your heartbreak will lead you where He means you to be. On that day, I don't think you'll wish you didn't experience the heartbreak. I think you'll be thankful that your God was there in the hurt, paving a way for the blessings you couldn't have imagined. Accept God's comfort, and be expectant of His blessings.

Dear God, I feel heartbroken and disappointed. But I know You will never disappoint me, and I can always rely on You. Nothing can separate me from Your love. Thank You for always being there for me. Help me trust You more and more. Amen.

8 AFFIRMATIONS FOR
OVERCOMING HEARTBREAK

1. YOUR HEART ISN'T BROKEN FOREVER. THE ONE WHO CREATED YOUR HEART WILL HEAL IT.

2. IT'S NOT A SIN TO CRY. JESUS IS NEAR THE BROKENHEARTED.

3. YOU'RE NOT CRAZY FOR BEING UPSET. YOU CARED, AND THAT'S GOOD.

4. LOOK FORWARD, NOT BACK.

5. YOU HAVE PEOPLE WHO CARE. PLAN SOMETHING FUN WITH A FRIEND.

6. THE FUTURE YOU IS THANKFUL FOR THE TWISTS AND TURNS.

7. IT'S A HARD CHAPTER, BUT THE STORY IS GOOD. JUST WAIT.

8. BLESSINGS ARE COMING. SAY GOODBYE TO THE DOORS THAT CLOSE, AND STAY EXPECTANT TO WHAT GOD IS GOING TO DO.

PRAYER CHANGES

OUR PERSPECTIVE.

TO THE GIRL STRUGGLING WITH MENTAL HEALTH

Fight the good fight of the faith. Take hold
of the eternal life to which you were called
when you made your good confession
in the presence of many witnesses.

—1 TIMOTHY 6:12

A few years ago, I went to the dentist and found out I had four cavities. They asked me if I had been smoking because I went from never having a cavity to having four. I have never smoked, but I did have a secret. My eating disorder had resurfaced, and this time I was making myself throw up regularly. I would not eat for a long time, then eat fast food, then make myself throw up because I felt ashamed by my lack of control.

I felt anxious and lonely, and overall, I was not in a good place. It was hard to find joy amid my struggle. This was after my first book on insecurity had come out, and I felt like a disappointment to my readers and the girls I led at church. I thought my mental health struggle made me unequipped to minister.

However, I finally did what I felt God calling me to do. I told one friend, and she pushed me to see a counselor. At counseling, I learned my mental health was going to be something I had to work at daily. I wasn't going to wake up and feel joyful overnight. But as I rooted myself in Christ again, I watched joy slowly blossom in my life, even as I continued through a season of struggling with my mental health.

Some of us have battles that we won't win until heaven. We have to fight daily. But these battles are worth fighting. Joy isn't just a gift we finally receive in heaven; it develops in our hearts when we root ourselves in Christ. Mental health can be a battle, but your Savior is fighting with you and for you. And that is a beautiful thing worth rejoicing over.

Are you like me? Do you fight for your mental health? One way to fight is to speak about what we're dealing with. To get better and find joy, we have to be honest about our struggles and be willing to fight through them. We will experience joy when we realize our Savior is near even when easy is far away.

Dear God, I pray for my mental health. Help me find peace, and give me the strength I need to fight and win. Remind me that joy doesn't come from an easy life but from knowing You are always near. Amen.

TO THE GIRL IN A RUSH

The simple believe anything, but the prudent
give thought to their steps.

—PROVERBS 14:15

One time when I was an intern, I had to lick envelopes and stuff an important letter in them. Easy, right? My friend and fellow intern, Logan, was in charge of writing the addresses because my handwriting is actually worse than a teenage boy's. So I was given the task of putting the letter in the envelope and licking it shut. Maybe it was due to my tongue feeling all weird, but somewhere along the way I started forgetting to put the letter in the envelope. And I had to awkwardly tell Logan what I did. But instead of being mad because I made our simple job harder, he laughed and said, "Okay, let's fix this."

If you're anything like me, you rush through your homework, your job, your day, or even a whole season of life. I've rushed through errands and forgotten something on my list, but I also missed an opportunity to meet a friend or make a stranger's day. Many of us have rushed to make friendships and ended up with friends who partied and not friends we had deep connections with. In our rush to feel accepted, we were left feeling lonelier than before. I've also seen friends rush through dating. Then problems come up years later because their partners don't know Jesus, and they realize they never waited for a good fit.

You can rush, or you can embrace. If you rush through everyday life, you'll miss out on joy. Joy isn't found by checking off a to-do list; it's found when you embrace the day God gives you and carefully take each step. In this busy world, it's hard to take each moment, day, and season slow. But you'll make life hard when you run toward the finish line of a task list and then have to start over the next day. Choose your hard. I would rather take the slow route filled with pit stops of God's blessings, opportunities, and joy than rush toward the next, right past God's goodness.

So to all the speedy girls out there: slow down. Take things off the list if you need to. You may be busy, but your peace needs to be a choice. Prioritize peace. Don't miss the most important part like I did when I didn't put that letter in the envelope. If slowing down seems impossible, ask God to share His priorities and perspective with you. He will give you the wisdom you need to walk at His pace and find joy in each step. Good times are ahead when you bring God's joy and timing with you. Joy isn't only to be found in your next. (Then there will be a new next!) Joy is right here in the journey of walking with the One who is planning your next.

Dear Jesus, help me to stop rushing, whether through the simple things or the hard things. Remind me to travel with the most important part of the journey—You and Your joy. Amen.

TO THE "GOOD" GIRL

For by grace you have been saved through faith.
And this is not your own doing; it is the gift of God,
not a result of works, so that no one may boast.

—EPHESIANS 2:8–9 ESV

In high school, some popular girls told me I was a "goody two-shoes." They were doing drugs and chasing boys, and I turned my homework in on time and didn't party. Their comments stung, and I felt like being a Christian was a burden. Obedience felt like a chore. Suddenly, volunteering wasn't fun, and I struggled to enjoy praying. I was also mad at God for not rewarding me for following His rules. One of the girls even got a boyfriend who loved Jesus. And she was at the top of our class—even though she cheated. Shouldn't I be rewarded for doing things right?

The truth is, I wasn't following Christ, I was following rules. I was a "good Christian," but I wasn't accepting Christ's love into my heart.

JESUS DOESN'T OWE YOU ANYTHING FOR BEING GOOD. In fact, He promised that His followers wouldn't fit in because the world's desires are at war with His desires (1 Peter 2:11). Following Christ's commandments won't make you popular. Being "good" doesn't mean you're promised a cute boyfriend or an easy career or *anything* from the world, but there is joy in following His good will.

Jesus told a story about two brothers. One left home and spent his dad's money partying. The other stayed and helped the family. When the party dude realized that his life wasn't fulfilling and returned home, the father celebrated his return. This made the "good" son upset. He had been working at home the whole time! But the father told him, "You are always with me, and everything I have is yours" (Luke 15:31). Jesus told this story to show that God celebrates hearts that seek Him, no matter the person's past.

Being good is a blessing when you realize it's about your good God. Don't be good for anything in return; be good because God has been good to you. Celebrate when good things happen to anyone, including those who aren't always good. Give grace to everyone, and remember that you have far greater blessings when you draw close to God and claim Him as your Savior. Your good works and good life won't save you. Only Jesus' death can do that. So don't be like the "good" son who had good works but no joy. Don't focus on whether life is going your way or not. Seek Christ and find a reason to celebrate.

Dear Father, remind me that obedience leads to Your joy. Give me a generous heart that celebrates others' blessings and doesn't get jealous when good things happen to those who have taken missteps. Thank You for saving me apart from anything I've done. Amen.

TO THE GIRL SEEKING CLOSURE

They will have no fear of bad news; their hearts
are steadfast, trusting in the LORD.

—PSALM 112:7

A guy I was dating for a couple of months ghosted me. He literally went from talking to me every day to silence. I remember realizing I was blocked and feeling crazy. Did I do something? What happened? How did he think it was okay to not even give me a conversation?

I tried three times to get closure from him. I wanted him to explain what changed and why things took a turn. He didn't respond. But three months later, he texted me something along the lines of, "Sorry I blocked you. I was in a hard place. How are you?"

I laughed. Three months before, I would have tried to get answers from him. But I didn't need closure from this boy anymore. See, after he ghosted me, I prayed to God. I was hurt. I was sad and disappointed. But then I remembered that I am worth more than the way this guy treated me. I stopped asking questions about what happened and started trusting God with this shut door. I realized it didn't matter why this boy had blocked me. He obviously wasn't God's best for me. Over time I found closure from knowing that God was leading me away from this guy. It didn't happen right away, but eventually, that answer was enough.

When you are left with unanswered questions, you won't find full closure from a text message, a meetup with an ex-friend, or a call with a family member. These things may answer some questions, but peace over a hard situation comes from knowing God's truths. Here are a few to get you started:

God is completely good (1 John 1:5).

He loves to give amazing things to His children (Matthew 7:11).

He isn't withholding blessings; He is preparing even greater things for you (Psalm 31:19).

God is preparing you to do good things for Him (Ephesians 2:10).

Instead of seeking "closure," seek to know God and find peace in who He is.

Dear God, remind me that true peace and closure come from knowing and trusting You. I have lots of questions, but I know that You are preparing good things for me. Help me to be steadfastly confident in Your plan for me. Amen.

6 REMINDERS FOR THE GIRL
READY TO WALK IN JOY

1. JOY ISN'T DEPENDENT ON YOUR CIRCUMSTANCES. JOY COMES FROM WHO YOU FOLLOW.

2. YOU CAN FIND MORE JOY IN RELATIONSHIPS THAT REFLECT JESUS.

3. YOU CAN SHARE JOY WITH OTHERS.

4. TAKING CARE OF YOURSELF MAKES YOU FEEL BETTER. BRUSH YOUR HAIR. PUT ON YOUR FAVORITE OUTFIT. GO FOR A WALK.

5. GOD IS ALWAYS UP TO SOMETHING GOOD. EXPECT GOOD IN YOUR DAY.

6. JESUS FEELS JOY WHEN YOU ARE NEAR HIM.

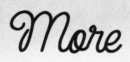

77

TO THE GIRL THINKING JESUS DOESN'T MAKE SENSE

Then he said to Thomas, "Put your finger here;
see my hands. Reach out your hand and put it
into my side. Stop doubting and believe."
Thomas said to him, "My Lord and my God!"
—JOHN 20:27-28

One day when I was seventeen, I cried to a mentor about my doubts. I wanted to believe that God was real. I wanted to believe that He was present and that Jesus rose from the dead. But let's be honest—it didn't make sense.

A couple of things about my life also didn't make sense: Why was I placed in a small town in Louisiana? Why did God let me go through that breakup? Why did I have to endure bullying in middle school? And why did God allow even worse things to happen to people around the world?

My mentor told me something powerful that day: Jesus came to save us, not to make sense.

Of course, the Bible can answer many questions. From the story of Adam and Eve, we see that bad things happen because sin broke the world that God created to be good. But that doesn't fully explain why *that* bad thing happened to you, and it's okay to wonder. You may never know why your parents got divorced or why you have a chronic illness. You may also not experience faith in the ways others do. You may never get chills during a worship song, and the stories in the Bible may always sound crazy. (A lot of them are!) But even in the doubts and questions, go to God. He is there. Be honest with Him. Ask your questions. Do you want Him to reveal Himself clearly to you? Ask Him. Do you want Him to show you how that hurt you faced can be used now for His glory? Ask Him. INSTEAD OF DEMANDING THAT GOD MAKE SENSE, GET TO KNOW HIM.

In the Bible, Thomas was a follower of Jesus. After Jesus rose from the dead, other disciples said they had seen Jesus alive. But Thomas doubted. He needed to see for himself. So Jesus showed Thomas the holes in His hands from the cross. Then Thomas replied, "My Lord."

I get that you want to see for yourself. Jesus didn't get down on Thomas for doubting; He showed Thomas His wounds. So don't just sit there questioning. Pray for God to show Himself to you. God cares about you and will give you what you need to believe. He might send you a friend, a mentor, a good song, or a scripture. Whatever happens, when you bring Him your questions, doubts, and concerns, you'll discover that He really is right there with you.

Dear heavenly Father, thank You for listening to my doubts and reaching me where I'm at. I ask that You reveal Yourself to me clearly. Help me have a heart that is eager to see You in my life. Amen.

78

TO THE GIRL FEELING UNWANTED

*Have mercy on me, my God, have mercy on me, for
in you I take refuge. I will take refuge in the shadow
of your wings until the disaster has passed.*

—PSALM 57:1

In tenth grade, I didn't get asked to homecoming. I didn't make the cheer team, and I got put in the back row of my dance recital. I also got my first C. Rough year, right?

Another time, I was chatting with this boy online. I was so excited that he wanted to talk to me—until I figured out it was a joke. I remember staring at my wall, unable to go to sleep, praying for God to let me be wanted for once in my life.

Fast forward to senior year: I won class president! I thought this victory in a big election would cure my feeling of being unwanted. I mean, I had friends, *and* a boy actually liked me! But the truth was, I still felt awful about myself. Even winning an important position and kissing a boy couldn't cure my insecurity.

During the time I was popular, I struggled with an eating disorder. Even after my first book came out (on insecurity!), I relapsed with my eating disorder. For months I made myself throw up after meals. The reality is that no matter what approval you get from this world—which lunch table you sit at or who you convince to like you—you won't feel worthy. Because your worth doesn't come from position or people.

See, I knew the right answers. I even wrote a book on the right answers! But I still struggled with feeling unwanted and unworthy. And maybe that's you. You've been told, "It doesn't matter. Let go and let God." But if you were honest with yourself, you still crave feeling wanted more than you crave Jesus.

The only way to feel worthy is to crawl under the shelter of God's wings. When you let Him love and affirm you, you will feel wanted and worthy no matter what the people around you say and do. Once you find refuge in Jesus and stop chasing worldly titles or rewards, you can find confidence in all seasons.

Dear God, I feel rejected and unwanted. I want to crawl under Your protection and let the rejection pass over me. Help me find confidence in being Your child. Thank You for wanting me close to You. Amen.

79

TO THE GIRL NEEDING ADVICE

How much better to get wisdom than gold,
to get insight rather than silver!

—PROVERBS 16:16

Before my first kiss, I did an embarrassing but common thing. I think everyone has done this, and if they say they haven't, they are probably lying. That's right. I googled how to kiss a boy. What was I thinking wikiHow was going to tell me? But I was so scared about that first kiss, so I sought advice—from Google.

Google did give me tips, but it didn't offer advice about whether I should actually kiss that boy. (I shouldn't have.) Had I looked for wisdom, it would have protected me from a hurtful decision.

But the truth is, I have done this way too many times. If you looked at my search history, you would see all sorts of weird queries:

how to lose five pounds quickly
what to do to make extra money fast
how to get into your dream college
how to respond to rumors about you
how to make friends

And of course . . . how to kiss a boy.

Many of the times that I went to Google, I was searching because I was scared. Maybe you're scared for college or your test next week. Or you're scared that girls are talking about you. Maybe your financial situation or your loneliness worries you. Often when we're afraid of the future, we try to figure it out ourselves. But when we type a quick search, ask the cool girl for advice, or "fake it till we make it," our fears turn into panic. And panic turns into recklessness.

You can't google wisdom, and you won't find answers inside your own efforts or feelings. When the future scares you, it is easy to search for answers from the world. But wisdom comes only from God.

So instead of panicking and rushing to Google, pray for wisdom. Then read God's Word. If you're scared about making new friends, follow the Bible's advice to spend time with other believers and try out a Bible study. If you're wondering whether you should break up with your boyfriend, read scriptures about love and find out if his love reflects God's love. The Bible can answer many of your fearful questions. And even more than that, God's wisdom shows that our lives are bigger than our worries. He helps us see what's important and what isn't worth our energy. When you need advice, don't sort through 3,258 results. Go to God for wisdom.

Dear God, I pray for wisdom. Lead me to seek truth from Your Word to answer my anxious thoughts. Help me walk in wisdom instead of acting from fear. Amen.

80

TO THE GIRL AFRAID OF A BORING LIFE

For all that is in the world—the desires of the flesh and the
desires of the eyes and pride of life—is not from the Father
but is from the world. And the world is passing away.

—1 JOHN 2:16–17 ESV

I spent the end of high school and first part of college trying my hardest to
have a "fun experience," which I thought meant partying. So I was thrilled
when I got asked to a fraternity formal. That meant I was living the best
college experience . . . right? But I knew what often happened afterward. I
remember thinking, *Oh wait, do I owe him a hookup?*

At this point, I was beginning to feel convicted for my party lifestyle.
However, I was scared that if I said yes to Jesus, I would have a boring life.
So I went to the formal. But I felt God reminding me over and over again
that I didn't owe this guy anything.

The night went pretty much how I thought. At first, this cute fraternity
guy flirted with me. But then he got upset at me for not sleeping with him
and slept with someone else. I was bummed. But I also had a realization:
this guy was not worth a crush. And for the record, you *never* owe a guy
anything.

Since then I've discovered that following Jesus isn't boring at all! I've learned to mountain bike, traveled to new states, and finally found some snow to make a snow angel. I've made amazing friends who will be my bridesmaids one day, and I even wrote some books.

Your life will look different when you're following Jesus, but you're not missing out. You're gaining something better than "fun" or a "normal" Friday night. You're gaining purpose, and you're living in God's protection from the pain sin brings. When I was partying, I was always bloated, woke up to cringey drunk texts and a headache, and even got in trouble with the police. None of that was fun or freeing.

True freedom doesn't come from driving away from your parents or going wild at a party. True joy isn't found when the cute boy asks you to the dance. True purpose doesn't come from living it up. True freedom, joy, and purpose come from realizing God gives you more than the world can offer. When you live with God, you get peace. Even when things go differently than you expect, you have hope for life after death. And you get true freedom to live an adventurous life following God. You're only missing out if you *don't* walk with Jesus.

Dear Jesus, I am struggling to trust that Your ways are better. But I know that I can find freedom, joy, and purpose only in You. Help me find fun friends who also want to live for You, and thank You for giving me something better than what the world offers. Amen.

81

TO THE GIRL FEELING INVISIBLE

She gave this name to the LORD who spoke to
her: "You are the God who sees me," for she said,
"I have now seen the One who sees me."

—GENESIS 16:13

I once had a friend who joked that she was invisible. Even at her own graduation, her name couldn't be heard because of the cheering for the girl in front of her. She told me this story with a sigh: "No one was listening for my name." She laughed about it, but she really hated this feeling.

I, too, have felt like no one, including God, was paying attention to me. My prayers have felt pointless. I've felt like God was seeing and hearing everyone but me. I've been mad at God for not answering my prayers.

Maybe you feel like no one listens to you. Or maybe you even feel like God doesn't hear your prayers. I know God feels distant sometimes, but He really is there. He isn't silent. He's at work writing you a better story than you could ever plan.

Hagar was a slave woman in the Bible who lived in the shadow of her mistress. She was abused and rejected, and she became pregnant by her master. When she ran away into the desert, God met her in her mess. He spoke to her and called her by name. This was powerful because, as she was a slave, it would have been rare for anyone to use her name. Then God blessed her. After this experience, Hagar called God "the God who sees me."

GOD SEES YOU AND LOVES YOU. Like Hagar, you may feel invisible to the world, but you're never invisible to God's eye. He sees your stress, your loneliness, your struggle. He may not be talking out loud or answering your prayers in the ways you want, but He's leading you out of your desert and blessing your future.

Sometimes we feel as if we're in the desert alone. We feel like no one sees us. But even if you think you have run away from it all, never forget there is a God who is on your side.

Knowing Jesus more means realizing that even when you have a lonely season or you feel overwhelmed and overlooked, you are never alone. There is a God in your desert. He won't leave you. When you know Jesus, you have a God who calls you by name and sees you.

Dear God, sometimes I feel like You don't listen to my prayers. But I know You are there. I know You see me when I'm locked in my room after a bad day, and I know You are listening to me as I pray. You are my Guide. Remind me to live a life that acknowledges Your presence. Amen.

82

TO THE GIRL WANTING TO HEAR GOD

*"Call to me and I will answer you, and will tell you great
and hidden things that you have not known."*
—JEREMIAH 33:3 ESV

I used to know a girl who would tell me how God spoke to her. I was so confused by Kayla talking about God this way. I was also jealous. What did He sound like? Why didn't I hear Him? I struggled with doubting that God was with me because I didn't hear His voice like Kayla did.

I desperately craved for Jesus to speak to me. Wouldn't it be easier if He proved to me that He was there? He seemed to do this for girls like Kayla. But I've learned that, in this thought process, I complicated His voice.

His voice isn't a literal whisper. Well, maybe He does that for some people. But His voice to me is a tug in my soul that pushes me to do something out of the ordinary for me. What some label a *conscience*, I label *Jesus*. His voice is found in my life situations, a friendly hug, and a journal entry where I realize that He protected me when I didn't get my way. When His voice comes into my thoughts, I know it isn't my own. It feels like peace amid chaos. His voice isn't audible, but it is real. There's no such thing as chance. That's Jesus.

And since you're reading this devotional, I bet you desire to know Scripture. The Bible was created by God to tell us who He is, what He has done, and what He will do. If you ever can't hear God, simply open your Bible and read the message He's already given you.

It's normal to doubt that God's voice is present in your life. It's okay to struggle to hear God. It's okay to have been a Christian for forever and wonder where God is. I've been there. However, you don't have to stay in this doubt. God's truth is stronger than any questions you have. Jesus is bigger than any doubt you have. God *is* speaking to you. But you need to learn how to listen. DON'T COMPLICATE HIS VOICE WITH YOUR EXPECTATIONS.

So on the nights you lie awake praying and wondering if God is there, listen. Look at your life circumstances and the people God has placed with you. Ask yourself if you already know the answer to your prayer. Open your Bible. Give God a chance to speak. It won't be a deep voice, but it will feel like peace. Trust that He will answer.

Dear God, I can't always hear You the way I want, but I trust that You're listening. Help me see You in the ordinary and find You even in the busy moments of life. Lord, use Your people, my circumstances, and Your Word to speak to me in ways more powerful than a voice. Amen.

5 WAYS TO HEAR GOD

1. READ THE BIBLE. SIT AT THE FEET OF JESUS AND LISTEN.

2. TURN OFF YOUR PHONE AND GO FOR A WALK.

3. LET GO OF YOUR EXPECTATIONS ABOUT THE WAY GOD SPEAKS TO YOU.

4. LOOK AROUND. GOD SPEAKS THROUGH FRIENDS, SOCIAL MEDIA POSTS, AND OUR SITUATIONS.

5. SERVE. TALK TO A FRIEND GOING THROUGH A HARD TIME, POUR INTO YOUNGER GIRLS, OR VOLUNTEER.

GOD'S VOICE FEELS LIKE

peace

IN THE MIDST OF CHAOS.

83

TO THE GIRL WANTING TO BE LIKE JESUS

When Jesus reached the spot, he looked up and
said to him, "Zacchaeus, come down immediately.
I must stay at your house today."

—LUKE 19:5

I worked at a restaurant for three years during high school. Being a wait-ress was hard, but I loved the people I worked with. There was one girl in particular I became close with. We shared music tastes, took fun pictures, cleaned up big messes by not-so-kind customers, and snuck into the back to eat dessert between shifts. And she wiped my tears after my first heartbreak. But we didn't have everything in common. She told me she didn't believe in Jesus because some Christians had hurt her.

Five years later, this friend messaged me after my first book came out: "Hey, Grace, it has been years since we worked together, and I see you're an author now. I am proud of you and always thankful for our times together. Because of you, I believe Christians aren't horrible. I still don't believe in Jesus, that's not my thing, but you're different. I know your faith makes you different, and one day I hope to have something like that."

I cried seeing this message. Even though she still didn't believe in Jesus, she had seen a bit of Him in me. My faith looked different to her because I shared it; I didn't push it. The Christian faith isn't just words or a story. Faith is the love of Jesus Christ. Jesus laughed with nonbelievers, and He ate with nonbelievers. When Jesus saw a man named Zacchaeus who had climbed a tree to get a view of Jesus, He told Zacchaeus to come down and take Him to Zacchaeus's house. Zacchaeus was a tax collector, a job known for stealing money. But Jesus invited him to spend time together, where Jesus could share a meal and a conversation, share an intimate moment, and share love.

Sometimes we make Christianity more complicated than it has to be. Some days, being like Christ starts with saying hello to someone with a bad reputation or a different religion or who is just different from you. Being a light starts by being present with the people in your life. You should have friends who don't believe in Jesus. And you should share the message of Jesus' sacrifice and what He's done in your life. But I hope you also share laughs, meals, tears, and stories. Sharing your heart and sharing your love is being Jesus. And don't forget to pray for your unbelieving friends. But most importantly, love them big.

Dear Jesus, I pray for my friends who don't believe in You. Help me share my faith in words but also follow Your example by sharing meals, stories, laughs, and tears. Soften their hearts and provide opportunities for me to talk about You in the conversations we share. Amen.

84

TO THE GIRL NOT FEELING GOD

Peter said to Jesus, "Lord, it is good for us to be
here. If you wish, I will put up three shelters—one
for you, one for Moses and one for Elijah."

—MATTHEW 17:4

One time I was in a worship session, and there was a girl on her knees with
her hands up. And her hands weren't just casually held in front of her; both
hands were reaching high, high. I think I even saw a tear come from her
eye. Other people had their hands up too. I remember thinking, *Why don't
I feel that way about Jesus?* I was at a point where Christ did not feel even
slightly close to me. So I wondered, *Is God just talking to them and not me?
Why am I not feeling it?*

I had felt Jesus before. I had gone to a youth camp, and He was so clear.
Maybe it was the mountains or the worship music, but I remember praying
and feeling peace. But then I went home . . . and I didn't feel God anymore.
I started wondering, *Was that really God I felt? Maybe it was the wind.*

Have you had an emotional experience with God and then felt like He
ghosted you? Or maybe you've never "felt Him" at all. Maybe you heard
someone yell an "Amen!" during a sermon and you didn't even understand

the point. Whatever the circumstances, you've noticed that others seem to feel it, get the goose bumps, and hear God while you're left feeling . . . normal.

WE'VE MADE FAITH TOO MUCH ABOUT FEELINGS. There's a story in the Bible that can help us understand why feelings aren't that important in faith. Peter, James, and John were with Jesus on a mountaintop when Jesus transfigured Himself, which means He revealed Himself as God. In excitement, Peter asked Jesus if they could build shelters on the mountain. Peter was having the biggest spiritual experience of His life, and he wanted to stay there. However, Jesus led them back down to the city, where He immediately cast out a demon. There was more work to be done.

Faith isn't about feelings. Faith is about serving Jesus when you aren't on a mountaintop. I hope you have moments when you feel like you're on the mountaintop with Jesus. But there will be more moments when school is overwhelming, your job feels too demanding, or you're distracted by heartbreak and loneliness, and you just don't feel Him. Please remember that God may not be shining in your face, but He's with you. He is always there, even when the feelings are not.

Dear Jesus, even though I don't feel You today, I will choose to walk with You. I know You are here because You are the same God who Peter saw on the mountaintop, and Your Word tells me that You are always present. Help me to walk with You consistently, even when I don't feel You. Amen.

85

TO THE GIRL UNSURE HOW TO PRAY

And being in anguish, he prayed more earnestly, and his
sweat was like drops of blood falling to the ground.

—LUKE 22:44

"Um . . . hi, God . . ." I'm pretty sure that's exactly what I said one night in college when I didn't know how to pray.

I had prayed when I was younger. Some had been genuine, heartfelt prayers, but others sounded like a list to Santa. "Dear God, I've been good, so can I have a boyfriend?" Now in college, I was over the party culture, but I felt stuck after a semester of ignoring God, drinking too much, and kissing frogs. Finally, I woke up hungover after blacking out (again) and realized I was at rock bottom. My prayer started off as awkward, but it turned into the most genuine prayer I had ever said. I came to Jesus honestly and broken and asked Him to help me. I remember being on my knees, asking God to change me.

Many people think that good prayers should be pretty. But I disagree. When Jesus was praying before He went to the cross, He was sweating blood. Now we know that sweating blood is a real condition that happens in the most stressful times. Jesus knew He was going to die a painful death on the cross. He even asked God if it was possible to not go through with it. His prayer wasn't pretty. It was emotional, real, pointed, and honest.

God wants your prayers to be real, not pretty.

I write down my prayers so I can go back and see how God has answered them. I don't try to say perfect words, I strive to have an honest heart. Sometimes that means I admit my pride, my hurt, my mistakes, my insecurity, my anger, my joy, and my doubt.

God doesn't want you to put your best foot forward when you pray. He wants honest prayers where you admit what you're feeling and experiencing. He wants your prayers even if you are so stressed out that your body is breaking down, like how Jesus was sweating blood. Don't try to craft beautiful prayers. Your Savior wants to hear from the real you. Be honest and consistent . . . and maybe even awkward.

Dear Jesus, You prayed when stressed and sweaty. Help me follow Your example and pray honestly. Prayer isn't about trying to be pretty; it's about coming to You with an honest heart. I will be bold and not be afraid of awkward and messy prayers. Amen.

86

TO THE GIRL DOUBTING THAT
JESUS CAN USE HER

Anyone who belongs to Christ has become a new
person. The old life is gone; a new life has begun!

—2 CORINTHIANS 5:17 NLT

I woke up after prom in a bed with my date. With him still asleep beside me, I cried. I didn't have sex, but I went further than I had ever gone before. I was also hungover, and I threw up shortly after. I'll never forget getting off the cold bathroom tile, looking at my reflection in the mirror, and thinking there was no way Christ could use this messy, sinful, broken girl. I was just about to lead a Bible study for younger girls, and I felt like maybe God was calling me to write Christian books. But now I felt like there was no way I could do those things.

Other choices in my past have also made me feel dirty and unqualified to live for Christ. I used to really struggle with being bold for Christ because my past felt too messed up. Aren't Christians supposed to have it all together and have a résumé of good deeds? I felt like all I had was a long list of failures, mistakes, flaws, frogs, and hungover messes.

But here's the truth . . . JESUS ISN'T FOCUSED ON YOUR PAST. He doesn't like that you chose sin over His best, but He doesn't expect perfection. He just wants you.

Paul's life shows that God can use people with even the most terrible pasts. After Jesus' death, Paul arrested Christians and helped kill them. But then he had a vision of Jesus. All of a sudden, he began preaching that Jesus was the Savior.

Did Paul mess up? Yes. But was the good news of Jesus more important than Paul's sins? Also yes. Paul dedicated his life to Jesus and traveled to different countries telling others about Him. The man who oppressed Jesus' followers went on to live a bold life for Christ.

Dear Jesus, I know I'm not the most qualified to talk about You and live for You, but I want to be like Paul. He wasn't perfect and even worked against You, but after He experienced You in a vision, He lived boldly for You. Use me, Lord, for Your will, even though I'm not qualified. I know Your love holds no record of wrongs. Help me experience conviction and walk away from sin and into a life that lives boldly for You. Amen.

87

TO THE GIRL FEELING REJECTED

He was despised and rejected by mankind, a man of suffering,
and familiar with pain. Like one from whom people hide their
faces he was despised, and we held him in low esteem.

—ISAIAH 53:3

Someone was trying to set me up with this cute guy. They showed me his picture, and I was down. He had a great smile, and rumor had it he served with middle school boys. He had a sweet mama and spoke highly of his little sister. He checked every box.

We met for coffee, and I liked him even more. However, he texted me the next day that he wasn't feeling it with me. He was kind, but he rejected me. I took it personally, and I tried to make him out to be a villain. I even listened to breakup songs, when really all that happened was a guy went to coffee with me and decided he didn't want to date me. This wasn't a crime or a sin, and it wasn't even supposed to be offensive.

One of my friends told me, "Grace, he wasn't feeling it, and there's nothing wrong with that. This rejection is better heard now." True. But it still felt awful.

Maybe you were rejected by a club, a sports team, a friend, a job, or a guy. I'm sorry. That sucks. But take a step back and look at the rejection again. This event is simply telling you that this isn't where you are meant to be. There doesn't need to be a villain in your story; there is a good God who can use this twist to lead you somewhere better.

If I could go back and tell myself anything after this coffee-shop boy, the cheer-team tryouts, the sorority rejection, the job layoff, or the friend desertion, I would say that joy can be found amid the unknown. Rejection is a reminder that you don't know your future, and that's not something to fear. You may not know where you are going or what life will throw at you, but you know you have a good God. If you've been rejected, there's something better in store.

Jesus knows what rejection feels like. He came to earth after God had been promising His people a Savior for thousands of years. But the Jews refused to believe in Jesus. And they didn't just reject Him—they murdered Him. Jesus' purpose wasn't to be invited, be cool, be liked, or get His way. His purpose was for His life to go God's way. He sacrificed His life so that we have a place in God's family.

Rejection hurts. But it's not the final answer on who you are or what you're worth. Tell Jesus about your pain, and know He's been there. Then look ahead.

Dear Jesus, my rejection hurts, but help me find joy. I know that You are using this closed door to lead me to something better. Amen.

TO THE GIRL AT ROCK BOTTOM

Praise be to the God and Father of our Lord Jesus Christ,
the Father of compassion and the God of all comfort, who
comforts us in all our troubles, so that we can comfort those in
any trouble with the comfort we ourselves receive from God.

—2 CORINTHIANS 1:3-4

As a college freshman, I got into the party scene. Drinking was what I did to mask my insecurity. I thought it would make my insecurity go away. But the alcohol only caused more destruction in my life. One night I went to a party with a new guy friend. I took a lot of shots and completely blacked out. A senior tried to take me to a room, and this guy friend stopped us and took me back to a couch. He gave me water and slept on another couch on the opposite side of the room. When I woke up in a panic that next morning, he drove me home and assured me nothing had happened to me. I later confirmed this. However, I remember sitting in my dorm room crying. Who had I become? What led me to living like this? Why was I running from God?

If you've ever been at rock bottom—whether struggling with the party scene, doing drugs to chase a high, or battling insecurity or depression—then you know that rock bottom is lonely, and it's hard to climb up. You can't see any light, and you feel stuck in the dark. But you aren't alone in the bottom of that black pit. Jesus is there too. And He isn't just watching you, shaking His head, waiting for you to get your crap together. He's a little like my freshman guy friend. When we are at rock bottom, Jesus is watching out for us, trying to protect us and care for us, and waiting for us to wake up the next morning and see that He is still there.

I know many girls have stories similar to mine that ended differently. If that is you, I'm sorry. But Jesus is by you right now. He wants to give you freedom and peace, and He's ready to wipe your tears.

Rock bottom feels horrible. But sometimes in rock-bottom situations, we wake up and notice our Savior's presence. He's there. He's with you, and He's ready to help you climb out of that pit and into His arms. Let Him take you home.

Dear Jesus, I am at rock bottom. I am in the darkness, and I need Your help to get out. Guide me toward Your light and away from the pain. Amen.

89

TO THE GIRL FEELING ALONE IN THE CROWD

The LORD God said, "It is not good for the man to
be alone. I will make a helper suitable for him."
—GENESIS 2:18

My loneliest moments have often been when I was surrounded by the most people.

My first day of high school, I searched for a familiar face before the bell. I didn't know where to stand or who to stand with. I went to a big school, and there were many people there. But I felt so lonely.

On prom night, everyone was dancing. Except me. I had only two friends at my school who really knew me. Even in a sea of people with T-Pain music playing, I felt lonely.

During college spring break one year, I went a little crazy with parties. As I stood next to the beautiful ocean surrounded by my sorority sisters, I felt more alone than ever.

Even now as I scroll on Instagram—despite followers and likes—I sometimes feel lonely.

Loneliness isn't a fun feeling, but loneliness is normal because God designed us to have a desire to be known. He didn't intend for people to be alone. But sometimes we choose to stay lonely and unknown. We choose to hide our feelings from others and God. And if no one knows an honest you, you will feel lonely. Allow loneliness to remind you that God wants you in relationships. And remember that you are not alone.

See, the cure to feeling alone isn't partying, going to college, posting TikToks, or being around more people. THE CURE TO LONELINESS IS REALIZING YOU ARE NEVER ALONE. The cure is having Jesus.

On the nights when you feel lonely and mornings when you wonder if you will be seen, remember that your Savior walks beside you. Maybe you feel alone because it seems that no one else doubts or struggles like you do. Or maybe you feel alone in your hurt. Maybe you are stuck in a friend group where no one cares about you honestly, or maybe your parents' divorce makes you feel like you don't have an actual bedroom.

You're going to make great friends one day, and you may have a moment when your TikTok gets seen by many people. Or you may even finally find good friends when you go to a different school. But loneliness will still arise. However, when you make your life about noticing God and not trying to be noticed, you'll find comfort and companionship in Him. Struggles will come, and friends may leave, but God is always with you.

Dear Father, I feel lonely. I know the cure to loneliness isn't a group of people or a party. The cure is knowing You. May I lean on You, and may You bless me with other people in my life who see me. My loneliness is real, but You are also real. Thank You for being here with me. Amen.

90

TO THE GIRL READY TO SHINE BRIGHT

"I am the vine; you are the branches. If you remain in me and I in you, you will bear much fruit; apart from me you can do nothing."

—JOHN 15:5

When I first accepted Jesus, I wanted to scream from the rooftops and announce to everyone what Jesus did in my heart. I thought that now that I was a Christian, I had to get busy for Him. I mean, the end times were coming! I needed to be loud for the gospel.

I talked about Jesus to everyone and anyone. Every status I posted on social media was all about Him. Because that's what good Christians do, right? But not long into this be-loud-for-Jesus campaign, I got burned out. I didn't feel Jesus anymore. I was talking *about* Jesus, but I forgot to talk *to* Jesus.

We want to shine bright for Jesus, so we get busy and get loud. But in our excitement, we forget what being a Christian is all about—being in a relationship with Jesus. We forget that we need to stay connected to Christ. Just like a light, we need a power source. We may shine our light for a little while on the energy that comes from a singular Jesus moment, like a camp, a good worship event, or a prayer time when you felt His presence. But if you don't stay plugged into God's Word, Christian community, and consistent prayer, your light will go out. Being consistent in your faith comes from getting to know God more and more, just like any relationship grows stronger as you spend time with that person. Learn Scripture, talk to God daily, and find people who point you to Him. If you only talk about God, but forget to talk *to* God, your light will fade.

Telling others about Jesus is wonderful, but make sure you are plugged into your faith daily too. As you experience more of God's power, you will be able to do more than just tell others about Jesus. You'll show them the difference He makes in your life. You will be a spotlight on His goodness because you are living in it every day.

Dear Jesus, thank You for being awesome! I want to shine bright for You. I know that to be a consistent light for You, worthy of others' trust, I need to talk to You more than I talk about You. Help me to seek You each day, stay consistent in my walk with You, and shine Your light. Amen.

7 REMINDERS FOR THE GIRL READY TO KNOW JESUS

1. JESUS IS WALKING WITH YOU RIGHT NOW. YOU DON'T NEED TO BOOK AN APPOINTMENT TO REACH HIM. JUST START TALKING.

2. JESUS VALUED WOMEN. IN A TIME WHEN WOMEN WERE OVERLOOKED AND LOOKED DOWN UPON, JESUS SAW WOMEN, LOVED WOMEN, AND CALLED WOMEN UP.

3. JESUS IS A COMFORTER. YOU WILL HAVE HARD DAYS, BUT YOU HAVE A COMPASSIONATE SAVIOR.

4. STORMS WILL COME, BUT YOUR SAVIOR CAN WALK ON WATER.

5. YOU ARE FORGIVEN. THE CROSS IS BIGGER THAN YOUR MISTAKES.

6. JESUS DOESN'T WANT YOUR PERFORMANCE OR "PERFECTION." HE WANTS YOUR HONEST HEART.

7. JESUS LOVES YOU. FOLLOWING JESUS IS MORE THAN A TICKET FOR HEAVEN. WITH HIS LOVE, THIS MESSY LIFE HAS PURPOSE.

ABOUT THE AUTHOR

GRACE VALENTINE is an author, blogger, podcast host, and speaker. Her readers love that she is young, ordinary, and relatable; they say her fresh voice helps them navigate their own faith and life. Grace's mission is to show others that Christianity is not lame—it is an adventure worth living.

Grace grew up near New Orleans, Louisiana, in a suburban town called Mandeville. She graduated from Baylor University in 2018 with a degree in journalism. She currently resides in Orlando, Florida, where she enjoys going on runs and eating lots of sushi. You can find Grace on Instagram @thegracevalentine; her podcast, *Water into Wine*; Twitter @GraceV96; or her website, GraceValentine.org. She is also a contributing writer for Proverbs 31 Ministries and Live Original. Grace loves connecting with her readers, so send her a message!

Grace is also the author of these titles:

From the Publisher

GREAT BOOKS

ARE EVEN BETTER WHEN THEY'RE SHARED!

Help other readers find this one:

- Post a review at your favorite online bookseller

- Post a picture on a social media account and share why you enjoyed it

- Send a note to a friend who would also love it—or better yet, give them a copy

Thanks for reading!

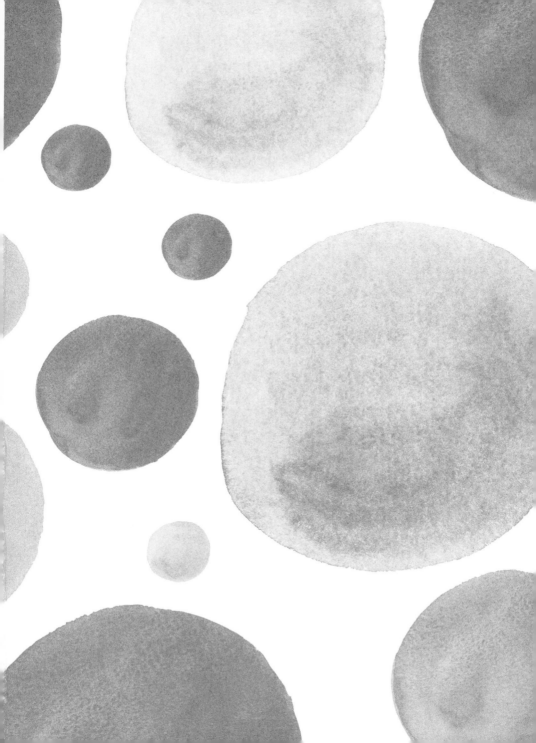